In the early part of the nineteenth century working people were quite powerless in the face of industrial, social and economic changes. They had no vote, and no voice in local or national government. But the Agrarian and Industrial Revolutions gave birth to the Labour Movement, to a working-class point of view and a desire to express that view.

This book is largely concerned with the "Self-help" movements which did so much to improve the living and working conditions for the mass of people in nineteenth-century Britain. Through a fascinating variety of contemporary writings—memoirs, Parliamentary reports and personal accounts—Geoffrey Morris traces the story of those working-class movements and their inspired leaders.

On next page A meeting of the unemployed in Hyde Park being broken up by the police.

The Rise of the Labour Movement

Geoffrey Morris

God is our Guide! From field, from wave,
From plough, from anvil and from loom,
We come, our country's rights to save,
And speak the tyrant faction's doom;
We raise the watchword Liberty—
We will, we will, we will be free.

A verse written by George Loveless, leader of the Tolpuddle Martyrs.

The Documentary History Series

THE COLD WAR *Elisabeth Barker*
THE COMMON MARKET *Elisabeth Barker*
THE THIRD REICH *Michael Berwick*
THE BLACK DEATH AND PEASANTS' REVOLT *Leonard Cowie*
THE REFORMATION OF THE SIXTEENTH CENTURY *Leonard Cowie*
THE PILGRIM FATHERS *Leonard Cowie*
PLAGUE AND FIRE *Leonard Cowie*
THE TRIAL AND EXECUTION OF CHARLES I *Leonard Cowie*
MODERN IRELAND *Alan Dures*
THE VIKINGS *Michael Gibson*
THE RISE OF JAPAN *Michael Gibson*
THE AMERICAN INDIAN *Michael Gibson*
RUSSIA UNDER STALIN *Michael Gibson*
WITCHCRAFT *Roger Hart*
ENGLAND EXPECTS *Roger Hart*
BATTLE OF THE SPANISH ARMADA *Roger Hart*
THE CRIMEAN WAR *Elizabeth Holt*
BLACK CARGO *Richard Howard*
THE BRITISH RAJ *Denis Judd*
MEDIEVAL PILGRIMS *Alan Kendall*
ITALY UNDER MUSSOLINI *Christopher Leeds*
THE UNIFICATION OF ITALY *Christopher Leeds*
BATTLE OF THE SOMME *Christopher Leeds*
THE RESTORATION *Douglas Liversidge*
THE JACOBITE REBELLIONS *Robert McKinnon*
THE MAKING OF AFRICA *Colin Nicolson*
ORIGINS OF WORLD WAR ONE *Roger Parkinson*
ORIGINS OF WORLD WAR TWO *Roger Parkinson*
ATTACK ON PEARL HARBOUR *Roger Parkinson*
THE SPANISH CIVIL WAR *Hugh Purcell*
THE AGE OF DICKENS *Patrick Rooke*
GLADSTONE AND DISRAELI *Patrick Rooke*
WOMEN'S RIGHTS *Patrick Rooke*
GUNPOWDER TREASON AND PLOT *Lewis Winstock*
THE GREAT DEPRESSION *Marion Yass*
THE HOME FRONT *Marion Yass*
HIROSHIMA *Marion Yass*

ISBN 0 85340 447 X

First published in England by Wayland Publishers Limited
49 Lansdowne Place, Hove, East Sussex, BN3 1 HF

Made and printed in Great Britain by
The Garden City Press Limited
Letchworth, Hertfordshire SG6 1JS

Contents

The Illustrations

An agricultural scene in pre-industrial England — ploughing, sowing and harrowing.

Introduction

Population

IN 1700 the population of England and Wales was a mere five and a half million. By 1801, the year of the first official census, it had risen to nine million. Fifty years later it had doubled to eighteen million. In the early eighteenth century the majority of English people lived in the rural South. The second half of the century, however, saw a gradual movement of people into the towns. One reason for this was that the factories of the industrial areas were able to offer the workers higher wages than those paid in agriculture.

The Enclosure Movement

The enclosure movement was a second reason for the flight of people from the countryside. Enclosure meant that small areas of common land were grouped together into larger farmed areas under one owner. Small peasant farmers were often driven from the land into the towns to seek work. Arthur Young, appointed Secretary of the Board of Agriculture in 1793, was a supporter of enclosures but had this to say about their effect on the poor: "By nineteen out of twenty enclosure bills the poor are injured, and some grossly injured . . . The poor in these parishes may say, and with truth, 'Parliament may be tender of property: all I know is that I had a cow, and an Act of Parliament has taken it from me' (1)." Many labourers were pushed off their land and lost the right to let their animals graze on the commons. Even if they were allowed to keep land, enclosure, with commissioners' fees, fencing and hedging, was a costly business. Understandably, riots against enclosure broke out quite frequently. For example, at Otmoor in Oxfordshire in 1814 "it was found impracticable to affix the Notices [of enclosures] on the Church doors, owing to large mobs, armed with every description of offensive weapons, having assembled for the purpose of obstructing the persons who went to affix the Notices, and who were prevented by violence, and threats of immediate death, from approaching the Churches (2)". Undoubtedly the enclosure movement worked to the advantage of the rich landowners who became richer, and to the disadvantage of many of the poor farmers who became poorer. A country rector writing at the end of the eighteenth century had this to say: "The landowner unites several farms into one. Thus thousands of families, which formerly gained an independent livelihood on those separate farms, have been gradually reduced to the class of day-labourers. But day-labourers are sometimes in want of work, and are sometimes unable to work; and in either case their resort is to the parish (3)."

Agricultural Labourers

William Cobbett, traveller, journalist, radical politician and writer of many works, noted the condition of agricultural labourers. This account of what he saw at Cirencester in 1821 was typical: "The labourers seem miserably poor. Their dwellings are little better than pig-beds, and their looks indicate that their food is not nearly equal to that of a pig. Their wretched hovels are stuck upon little bits of ground *on the roadside* where the space has been wider than the road demanded. In many places they have not two rods to a hovel. It seems as if they had been swept off the fields by a hurricane, and had dropped and found shelter under the banks on the roadside. In my whole life I never saw human wretchedness equal to this (4)."

The great changes in industry, which we call the Industrial Revolution, took place between 1760 and 1860. The introduction of new machinery into the large factories meant the decline of the cottage industries. Like the changes in agriculture (known as the Agrarian Revolution) the Industrial Revolution accelerated the growth of towns. In addition the concentration of workers in towns and large factories made the working classes, or the proletariat, conscious of their class and its struggles. They began to realize that only by unity and self-help could they hope to improve their position in relation to other classes. Thus the Industrial and Agrarian Revolution gave birth to the Labour Movement, to a working-class point of view. To working-class organizations, they gave the desire to express that point of view.

Factory Conditions

Life in many domestic industries had been harsh and hard. In the industrial factories and workshops, conditions of work were much worse. There was poor light and little fresh air, unguarded machines, and harsh overseers. Men, women and children worked long hours, often for poor wages. In 1800 there were no legal regulations for hours and conditions of work, and no binding agreements on wages. The workers were forbidden by law to form trade unions. There was no compensation for injury, no old age pension, no unemployment pay or sickness pay. Parents were often forced to send children to work as they themselves were unemployed and were refused parish relief if they had children who could work. As late as 1833 we have this story of child labour: "I am now sixteen years of age. I have been employed in piecing at a worsted mill. I entered the mill at nine years of age; my father was obliged to send me to the mill in order to keep me. If we are higher than the frames we have to bend our bodies and our legs. I had worked about a year for those long hours before I found my limbs began to fail. The failing came on with great pain in my legs and knees (5)."

Conditions in the textile factories were particularly forbidding, William Cobbett tells how "Some of these lords of the loom have in their employ thousands of miserable creatures. In the cotton-spinning work, these creatures are kept, fourteen hours in each day, locked up, summer and winter, in a heat of from eighty to eighty-four degrees . . . Observe, too, that these

Children at work in a textile mill around 1835.

On facing page The back-to-back houses of the poor.

poor creatures have no cool room to retreat to, not a moment to wipe off the sweat, and not a breath of air to come and interpose itself between them and infection . . . In addition to the noxious effluvia of the gas, mixed with the steam, there are the dust and what is called cotton-flyings or fuz, which the unfortunate creatures have to inhale (6)."

Conditions in the Mines

Conditions in other industries, notably pottery, and iron and steel, were also dangerous to health. It was down the mines, however, that conditions were worst, especially for women and children. The following was a typical example of evidence given by a girl aged thirteen: "I went into a pit to help before I was five years old. I used to thrust; I didn't do it long. I hurry now with a belt and chain in the broad-gates. There are no rails there. We have to hurry full corves [coal-miners baskets] this way, up hill as well as down. I do this myself, and I have 26 runs a day. There are girls that hurry in the same way, with belt and chain. Our breeches are often torn between the legs with the chain (7)."

Young children who worked long hours down the mines only saw daylight on Sundays during the winter months. An eight-year-old girl's story goes: "I'm a trapper in the Gauber Pit. I have to trap without a light, and I'm scared. I go at four and sometimes half-past three in the morning, and come out at five and half-past. I never go to sleep. Sometimes I sing when I've light, but not in the dark; I dare not sing then. I don't like being in the pit. I am very sleepy when I go sometimes in the morning (8)."

Hauling coal underground, from *The Coal Commission Report* of 1842.

Housing Conditions

In the mining and industrial districts housing conditions were particularly bad at the beginning of the nineteenth century. Drainage of sewage, and the provision of fresh water supplies, were often non-existent. The houses were built "back-to-back." They lacked ventilation, and had shared privies in the courts and alleyways; disease was rampant. Many thousands of city dwellers lived in cellars. This was true of Manchester as early as 1795: "In some parts of the town, cellars are so damp as to be unfit for habitation . . . The poor often suffer from the shattered state of cellar windows (9)." Of the same city, it was written in 1832: "The greatest portion of those districts inhabited by the labouring population . . . are untraversed by common sewers. The houses are ill-soughed [drained], often ill-ventilated, unprovided with privies, and in consequence, the streets which are narrow, unpaved, and worn into deep ruts, become the common receptacle of mud, refuse and disgusting ordure . . . The state of the streets powerfully affects the health of the inhabitants (10)."

In *The Old Curiosity Shop* (1841) Charles Dickens described the new industrial landscape: "On mounds of ashes by the wayside, sheltered only by a few rough boards, or rotten penthouse roofs, strange engines spun and writhed like tortured creatures; clanking their iron chains, shrieking in their rapid whirl from time to time as though in torment, unendurable, and making the ground tremble with their agonies. Dismantled houses here and there appeared, tottering to the earth, propped up by fragments of others that had fallen down, unroofed, windowless, blackened, desolate, but yet inhabited. Men, women, children, wan in their looks and ragged in attire, tended the engines, fed their tributary fires, begged upon the road, or scowled from the doorless houses."

The Rich and the Poor

Another novelist, the future statesman Benjamin Disraeli, gave his fourth novel *Sybil* (1845), the sub-title "The Two Nations." In it he described the deep social and economic divisions caused by the Industrial Revolution: "Two Nations; between whom there is no intercourse and no sympathy . . . who are formed by different breeding, are fed by different food, are ordered by different manners, and are not governed by the same laws . . . THE RICH AND THE POOR."

The poor in London: an old man selling flowers.

The Influence of the American and French Revolutions

The worker in the early part of the nineteenth century had every right to feel powerless against the changes that were taking place. Workers had no vote, and no voice in local or national government. People had to own land before they could stand for election to Parliament. In the country areas ownership of land decided whether a person could vote or not. However, the workers had been inspired by the ideals and achievements of the Americans, in their War of Independence (1776–83), and the French, in their Revolution (1789). The Americans had said that "Life, Liberty and the pursuit of Happiness" are "inalienable rights," and that "whenever any form of government becomes destructive of these ends, it is the Right of the People to alter, or to abolish it, and to institute new Government." The French in their Declaration of the Rights of Man had said: "Men are born and remain free and equal in rights . . . These rights are liberty, property, security and resistance to oppression . . . Law is the expression of the general will. All citizens have the right to take a part personally, or through their representatives in its formation."

To members of the working class in Britain these declarations offered hope and freedom; but to the ruling authorities they brought fear of resistance and rebellion. The scene was set for a long and often bitter class struggle in nineteenth-century England.

Peasants taking to arms during the French Revolution of 1789.

1 Riots and Rebels

MEN OF ALL CLASSES in Britain were deeply affected by the French Revolution. Many reform societies were set up. One society wrote in a letter of congratulation to the French in 1789: "The Society for Commemorating the Revolution in Great Britain, disdaining national partialities and rejoicing in every triumph of liberty and justice over arbitrary power, offer to the National Assembly of France their congratulations on the Revolution in that country, and on the prospect it gives to the two first kingdoms in the world, of a common participation in the blessings of civil and religious liberty."

Reform Clubs

However, after the Revolution in France, there was a Reign of Terror. This frightened a large section of the English public, and cooled the enthusiasm of many reformers, but the cause remained alive. Pitt's Government thought that reform clubs and societies were likely to bring rebellion. Legislation was passed against them after England had declared war on France in 1793. The Government hired spies to report on the activities of the societies, and some of these reports were alarming. However, there is no real evidence that the societies wanted violence or mob rule, and it may well be that the spies were "touching up" the evidence to please their paymasters.

The London Correspond-ing Society

At first, the reform clubs of the 1790s had a middle-class leadership, but this element declined as the attacks on them grew. It is difficult to estimate the strength, influence, numbers and activities of the reform societies. This was because many were secretive, and others chose to go "underground" rather than risk prosecution. The London Corresponding Society was the first real working-class independent organization. Its members were respectable working men who had been deeply moved by the hardness of the times in which they lived. Their hopes had been raised by the French Revolution and they wished to join in the demand for political reforms. Their main requests were for

On facing page A street battle in Liverpool: strikers fight with the police.

Tom Paine, author of *The Rights of Man*.

universal suffrage (the vote for everyone) and annual parliaments. They organized themselves on the Methodist model of "classes" for discussion, and issued pamphlets and addresses. Most of the members were skilled craftsmen, and the ideas they put forward were expressed by Tom Paine. In 1791–92, he published his book *The Rights of Man*, in which he defended the French revolutionaries on the ground that they had every right to set themselves free from an evil government. He wrote: "I do not believe that monarchy and aristocracy will continue seven years longer in any of the enlightened countries in Europe. If better reasons can be shown for them than against them, they will stand; if the contrary, they will not. Mankind are not now to be told that they shall not think or they shall not read; and publications that go no further than to investigate principles of government, to invite men to reason and to reflect and to show the errors and excellencies of different systems, have a right to appear."

Cartoon showing Ned Ludd dressed as a woman.

The Sheffield Society

A reform club in Sheffield issued free copies of Tom Paine's writings. The club had a harmless enough name—The Sheffield Society of Constitutional Information, giving the impression almost of an educational society rather than one modelled on a French Revolutionary Club. When it organized marches and demonstrations, however, banners and placards had such slogans as: "Rights of Man" and "Liberty" and "Franchise." There were some six hundred members of the Sheffield Society, each paying 1d (one old penny, about ½p) a week subscription (another Methodist influence). The local press estimated that 10,000 people attended some of the demonstrations.

The Luddites

Before the French Wars ended in 1815, however, the most serious riots were directed towards machine-wrecking. The mechanization of industry meant that the livelihood of hand workers was increasingly threatened. In 1810 the master hosiers in the Nottinghamshire hosiery trade lowered wages and began to make stockings on wider frames. The wider material was not shaped in the making, but cut up afterwards and sewn into stockings. These machines could make larger quantities of lower grade stockings than the narrower frames. As there was already over-production in the industry, this meant that fewer men were needed. The result was that in 1811 and 1812 bands of workmen went around smashing up frames which made "cut-ups" and issuing letters signed by King Ludd or Ned Ludd. This gave the name Luddite to the riots and rioters. Machine-breaking soon spread to other areas; the Lancashire Luddites were hand-loom weavers, and the Yorkshire Luddites were croppers. Croppers were highly skilled shearmen who cut the nap off the woollen cloth. They hated the new shearing frames bought by the factory owners which did the work of four men, and threatened employment. In many areas in the Midlands and North there was widespread and prolonged destruction of machinery by midnight raids of masked and often armed men. Factory owners often received threatening letters, such as this one sent to a Huddersfield factory owner in 1812: "Sir, Information has just been given in, that you are a holder of those detestable shearing frames, and I was desired by my men to write to you, and give you fair warning to pull them down . . . that if they are not taken down by the end of next week, I shall detach one of my lieutenants with at least 300 men to destroy them and further more take notice that if you give us the trouble of coming thus far, we will increase your misfortunes by burning your buildings down to ashes, and if you have the impudence to fire at any of my men, they have orders to murder you and burn all your Housing. You will have the goodness to go to your neighbours to inform them that the same Fate awaits them if their Frames are not taken down . . . Signed by the General of the Army of Redressers, Ned Ludd (11)."

In 1812 Parliament made frame-breaking a hanging offence, but the riots continued under cloak of great secrecy. Luddites bound themselves by taking oaths such as this one:

Luddite Oath

"I, A.M., of my own voluntary will, do declare and solemnly swear, that I never will reveal to any person or persons under the canopy of heaven, the names of the persons who compose this secret committee, their proceedings, meetings, places of abode;

dress, features, complexion or anything else that might lead to a discovery of the same, either by word, deed, or sign, under the penalty of being sent out of the world by the first brother who shall meet me, and my name and character blotted out of existence, and never to be remembered but with contempt and abhorrence; and I further now do swear, that I will use my best endeavours to punish by death any traitor or traitors, should any rise up among us, whenever I can find him or them, and though he should fly to the verge of nature, I will pursue him with unceasing vengeance. So help me God and bless me to keep this my oath inviolable (12)."

The shooting and killing of two Yorkshire mill-owners lost the Luddites the sympathy of many of the working class. It also increased the determination of the authorities to round up the Luddite leaders. Before the end of 1812 sixty-four men were being held in York Castle, awaiting trial for various offences in the Luddite disturbances. Thirty-eight of the accused were there on capital charges. The prospects for the croppers were bleak. With the subduing of the leaders, the riots became more irregular. More and more mill-owners installed the new machinery, which inevitably led to more unemployment. Derbyshire, Leicestershire and Cheshire also witnessed Luddite rioting, until 1816. The Luddites made up a negative and often violent protest movement, which failed to achieve its real objective.

The machine-wreckers attacking the house of John Kay the inventor of the flying shuttle.

On facing page The Peterloo Massacre, cavalry attacking the crowds gathered in St Peter's Fields, Manchester.

However, the movement succeeded in binding working people together in a desperate comradeship, with an intense hatred of, and opposition to, the ruling classes. The song of the cropper lads typified their spirit:

Some cropper lads of great renown
Who love to drink good ale that's brown
And strike each haughty Giant down,
With hatchet, pike and gun.
O, the cropper lads for me,
And gallant lads they be,
With lusty stroke the shear frames broke,
The cropper lads for me.

What though the specials still advance,
And soldiers nightly round us prance,
The cropper lads still lead the dance,
With hatchet, pike and gun!
And night by night when all is still
And the moon is hid behind the hill,
We forward march to do our will
With hatchet, pike and gun! (13)

In the years following the end of the Napoleonic Wars there were several isolated outbreaks of protest. The 1815 Corn Law and the bad harvests between 1816 and 1819 made bread dearer. There was widespread unemployment, and understandably, there was distress and discontent. In 1816 there were riots in Spa Fields in London. The Government was forced to suspend the Habeas Corpus Act which enabled imprisonment without trial. In the following year the Gagging Acts were passed, which forbade public meetings except under licence from magistrates. In 1817 there was the "March of the Blanketeers." Cotton workers from Lancashire set out to march to London to present a petition to the Prince Regent. They got their name from the blankets which they carried with them to sleep in on the way. The march was broken up by local soldiers. In 1817 the Derbyshire Insurrection took place. Unemployed framework knitters, deliberately stirred up by a notorious government spy named

Oliver, were forcibly dispersed and their leaders hung, drawn and quartered at Derby gaol. Two years later, in 1819, a mass meeting was called at St Peter's Fields, Manchester. A leading radical, Henry Hunt, was to be the main speaker. An orderly but vast crowd assembled, holding flags ". . . with various mottoes, such as 'No Corn Laws,' 'Liberty or Death,' 'Taxation without representation is Tyranny,' 'We will have Liberty.' Information was brought to Mr Hunt that St Peter's Field was already filled, and that no less than 300,000 people were assembled . . ."

The "Peterloo Massacre"

"Mr Hunt began his discourse by thanking them for the favour conferred on him, when a cart, which evidently took its direction from that part of the field where the police and magistrates were assembled in a house, was moved through the middle of the field to the great annoyance and danger of the assembled people, who quietly endeavoured to make way for its procedure. The cart had no sooner made its way through, when the Yeomanry Cavalry made their appearance from the same quarter as the cart had gone out . . . The Yeomanry Cavalry made their charge with a most infuriate frenzy; they cut down men, women and children, indiscriminately, and appeared to

Henry Hunt, President of the Peterloo meeting.

have commenced a premeditated attack with the most insatiable thirst for blood and destruction (14)."

Over 400 people were wounded, 113 being women. Eleven died, including two women and a child. After the event Lord Sidmouth, the Home Secretary, sent a letter of congratulation to the Manchester authorities. The massacre drew protests from all classes of society, including much bitter verse:

And the heroic host no more shall boast
The mighty deeds of Waterloo,
But this henceforth shall be the toast
The glorious feats of Peterloo!

Samuel Bamford, a Lancashire weaver-poet, wrote *A Song of Slaughter* which included:

Ah, behold their sabres gleaming,
Never, never known to spare.
See the floods of slaughter streaming!
Hark the cries that rend the air!

Youth and valour nought availed!
Nought availed beauty's prayer!
E'en the lisping infant failed
To arrest the ruin there!

Give the ruffians time to glory!
Theirs is but a waning day;
We have yet another story
For the pages of history (15).

Far from giving in, the Government stiffened its attitude still further. In 1819 it passed the Six Acts. Some of these Acts were aimed at preventing unauthorized carrying of weapons and military training and were quite sensible. Some, however, aimed to prevent publication of pamphlets and only increased popular resentment. This culminated in the Cato Street Conspiracy of 1820, when an attempt to murder the entire Cabinet by a few fanatics was fortunately discovered and prevented. The radicals, led by Arthur Thistlewood, were arrested in Cato Street, off the Edgware Road in London. Five of them were hanged and five transported for life. The poet Shelley reacted sharply to the Six Acts:

"To the Men of England, 1819."

Men of England, wherefore plough
For the Lords who lay ye low?
Wherefore weave with toil and care
The rich robes your tyrants wear?

The seed ye sow another reaps;
The wealth ye find another keeps;
The robes ye weave another wears;
The arms ye forge another bears.

Sow seed—but let no tyrant reap;
Find wealth—let no imposter keep;
Weave robes—let not the idle wear;
Forge arms—in your defence to bear.

The Swing Rioters

Between 1826 and 1832 the Swing Riots took place in southern, agricultural England. The state of the rural poor was terrible. Examples of poaching, rick-burning, cattle maiming, sheep stealing and machine-breaking began to spead. Threatening letters signed by "Captain Swing" were sent to landowners and

Rick-burning in Kent in the 1830s.

farmers. The riots were at their height in 1830. They stretched from Kent to Dorset, and included East Anglia and the South Midlands. The labourers demanded higher wages, and higher rates of poor relief, together with a lowering of rents. Some magistrates clearly felt that the labourers had a case. In 1870 Norfolk magistrates wrote that the "disturbances principally arise from the use of Threshing Machines, and to the insufficient Wages of the Labourers. The Magistrates therefore beg to recommend to the Owners and Occupiers of Land in these Hundreds, to discontinue the use of Threshing Machines and to increase the Wages of Labour to Ten Shillings a week for able bodied men, and that when task work is preferred, that it should be put out at such a rate as to enable an industrious man to earn Two Shillings per day.

"The Magistrates are determined to enforce the Laws against all tumultuous Rioters and Incendiaries, and they look for support to all the respectable and well disposed part of the Community; at the same time they feel a full Conviction, that no severe measures will be necessary, if the proprietors of Land will give proper employment to the Poor on their own Occupations, and encourage their Tenants to do the same (16)."

Cartoon of the Duke of Wellington addressing one of his captives during the Swing Riots

Some Berkshire magistrates later in the same year, having gained some support from local farmers, urged the agricultural labourers to work peacefully: "To the Labouring Classes. The Gentlemen, Yeomanry, Farmers, and others, having made known to you their intention of increasing your Wages to a satisfactory extent; and it having been resolved that Threshing Machines shall not be again used; it is referred to your good Sense that it will be most beneficial to your own permanent Interests to return to your usual honest occupations, and to withdraw yourselves from practices which tend to destroy the Property from whence the very means of your additional Wages are to be supplied. Hungerford, 22nd November, 1830 (17)."

Machine-breaking and burning continued until at least 1832. The authorities took brutal steps to punish the guilty; nine men were hanged and some 450 transported, many more were imprisoned. The Duke of Wellington himself boasted of having hunted down Hampshire rioters like game or cattle; he wrote: "I induced the magistrates to put themselves on horseback, each at the head of his own servants and retainers, grooms, huntsmen, game-keepers, armed with horsewhips, pistols, fowling pieces and what they could get, and to attack in concert, if necessary, or singly, these mobs, disperse them, and take and put in confinement those who could not escape. This was done in a spirited manner, in many instances, and it is astonishing how soon the country was tranquillized."

The Swing rioters had more success than the Luddites. Threshing machines were not bought on a large scale, and labourers' employment was safeguarded and some wages raised.

The National Union of the Working Classes

The first really positive and non-violent working-class organization was set up in 1831. It was known as The National Union of the Working Classes, but tended to be restricted in its activities to meetings of intelligent London craftsmen. The movement was strongly influenced by Tom Paine's writing which had campaigned for everyone's right to political liberty and equality, and the right to the full enjoyment of the products of their labour. The political aims of the movement included annual parliaments, manhood suffrage, vote by ballot and no property qualification for MPs. Like the reform clubs of the 1790s, the members of the National Union of the Working Classes organized themselves like the Methodists: "The whole of the members of the association divide themselves into classes, after the manner of the Wesleyan Methodists, that each class has, after the manner of those Methodists, what is called a 'leader,' who collects the contributions, pays the expenses, and manages the business of the class (18)."

Reform Riots

In October 1831, the House of Lords rejected the Reform Bill and at once serious disturbances broke out in various parts of the country, especially Nottingham, Derby and later in Bristol. In Nottingham considerable rioting ended in the burning down of the castle, the property of the Duke of Newcastle. In Bristol "the mansion house, custom house, excise office and Bishop's Palace were plundered and set on fire; the toll gates pulled down; the prisons burst open with sledge hammers (19)." The National Union of the Working Classes attempted to call a meeting to demand, among other things, the abolition of hereditary privilege, but the Government prohibited the meeting.

The Reform Bill, when it was passed in 1832, was a great disappointment to the Labour Movement. The working class gained no immediate benefit from it; the political gains went to the middle class. Working-class people were still without the vote.

An old reform banner of 1832.

Leading Chartists and the causes they stood for.

2 Charter and Chartists

CHARTISM HAS BEEN described as the first great political working-class movement in the world. It all began with the London Working Men's Association, founded in 1836. Its secretary was a cabinet maker named William Lovett. The object of the Association was "to draw into one bond of unity the intelligent and influential portion of the working classes in town and country, and to seek by every legal means to place all classes of society in possession of equal political and social rights." Membership was limited to working men, although sympathizers from other classes could be honorary members. In 1837 the Association, in conjunction with a group of radical MPs, drew up the People's Charter which had six demands.

The Charter

1 A vote for every man twenty-one years of age, of sound mind, and not undergoing punishment for crime.
2 The ballot. To protect the elector in the exercise of his vote.
3 No property qualification for Members of Parliament —thus enabling the constituencies to return the man of their choice, be he rich or poor.
4 Payment of Members of Parliament, thus enabling an honest tradesman, working man, or other person, to serve a constituency, when taken from his business to attend to the interests of the country.
5 Equal constituencies, securing the same amount of representation for the same number of electors—instead of allowing small constituencies to swamp the votes of larger ones.
6 Annual parliaments, thus presenting the most effectual check to bribery and intimidation, since though a constituency might be bought once in seven years [even with the ballot], no purse could buy a constituency [under a system of universal suffrage] in each ensuing twelve month; and since Members when elected for a year only, would not be able to defy and betray their constituents as now (20).

Richard Oastler.

John Fielden.

The Charter soon attracted support, particularly in the industrial North and Midlands. The movement was strong both in areas where industry was decaying and where it was rapidly expanding. The weakest areas were villages and market towns. The first phase of Chartism was bound up with the agitation for factory reform, particularly the Ten Hours Movement, and with the struggle against the new Poor Law. John Fielden, himself a factory owner, and Richard Oastler, a Yorkshireman, led this dual campaign. Oastler's famous letter to the *Leeds Mercury* included these words: "Thousands of our fellow-creatures and fellow-subjects, both male and female, the miserable inhabitants of a Yorkshire town, are this very moment existing in a state of slavery, more horrid than are the victims of that hellish system colonial slavery (21)."

Some causes of Chartism

The Poor Law Amendment Act of 1834 set out to abolish the system of subsidizing wages and all forms of outdoor relief for the able-bodied. In their place were substituted "deterrent" workhouses, in which man and wife were separated, and life made deliberately harsh and hard. Anti-Poor Law Associations were formed to organize resistance, but most of them merged later into the local Chartist organizations. Bronterre O'Brien, editor of *The Poor Man's Guardian*, wrote in 1833 that "a spirit of combination has grown up among the working classes of which there has been no example in former times . . . They aspire to be at the top instead of the bottom of society—or rather that there should be no bottom or top at all." There is other contemporary evidence of a growing working-class point of view; a parliamentary committee reported in 1835:

"Question: Are the working classes better satisfied with the institutions of the country since the change [the Reform Bill of 1832] has taken place?

Answer: We do not think they are. They viewed the Bill as a measure calculated to join the middle and upper classes to Government, and leave them in the hands of the Government as a sort of machine to work according to the pleasure of Government (22)."

The *Annual Register* of 1839 described Chartism as "an insurrection which is expressly directed against the middle classes." Certainly those Chartists who were free traders would have nothing to do with the Anti-Corn League because they believed it to be a middle-class movement, and indeed some of the League's meetings were broken up by Chartists. Some fringe Chartists earned a bad name for their movement by their excesses at League meetings. At Huddersfield in March 1839, the action of the Chartists (complained one free trader) "was such as to excite the unmitigated disgust of every well-regulated mind, and to us it is a matter of perfect astonishment how a body of Englishmen can be found so utterly lost to all sense of decency, and so determinedly opposed to candour, honesty, and fair-dealing. Everything in the shape of argument or appeal to facts was denounced as lies—the most ribald abuse of the speakers was indulged in, and they were clamoured down by hooting, hissing, stamping on the floor, and every other species of unmanly arrogance (23)."

Some women's organizations threw their support behind the Chartists. The Newcastle upon Tyne Female Political Union, for example, issued this appeal: "Fellow-Countrywomen. We call upon you to join us and help our fathers, husbands, and brothers, to free themselves and us from political, physical and mental bondage, and urge you to [help] pass the people's Charter into a law and emancipate the white slaves of England. This is what the working men of England, Ireland and Scotland are struggling for . . . (24)."

National Convention

Chartist mass meetings were held throughout the country in 1839. The movement recruited best where Luddism had gone before. Birmingham was one such area. There, middle-class leaders such as Thomas Attwood, a banker and MP, and Joseph Sturge, a wealthy Quaker corn merchant, were prominent. It was also from Birmingham that a suggestion came to send a great national petition to Parliament, asking for the immediate adoption of the Charter. Early in 1839 a Chartist National Convention assembled in London with Lovett as secretary; it was called the "General Convention of the Industrious Classes" or the "People's Parliament". Some of its members wrote after their names "MC"—"Member of the Convention". The Convention prepared a petition for Parliament. It had been signed by one and a quarter million people; it weighed six hundredweight, was two miles long and was placed on a huge wagon decorated with banners.

The First Petition

In Parliament "Mr T Attwood said in rising to present this very extraordinary and important petition . . . [that] he held in his hand a list of two hundred and fourteen towns and villages, in different parts of Great Britain, where the petition had been deliberately adopted and signed; and it was now presented to the House with 1,280,000 signatures, the result of not less than 500 public meetings. At each of those meetings there had been one universal anxious cry of distress—distress which had caused much discontent amongst the working people, and which discontent was created by the long sufferings and grievances which that class of the people had endured, and so long utterly disregarded by the people's representatives in that House [order, order] (25)."

The Petition was rejected by the Commons by 235 votes to 46. The Convention then proclaimed a general strike, a so-called "Sacred Month," but later cancelled it. However, there were Chartist demonstrations and riots in various parts of the country. Disturbances in the Bull Ring in Birmingham were severely handled by London police sent for the purpose. Lovett himself was arrested there.

The Monmouth Rising

In Newport, Monmouthshire, a large mass of Chartist miners led by John Frost, an ex-mayor of the town, marched on the gaol in an attempt to release an imprisoned Chartist leader, John Vincent. The spirit of the marchers can be seen in this letter by a young recruit to the Chartist cause.

On facing page Chartist rioters attack a workhouse in Stockport.

Thomas Attwood.

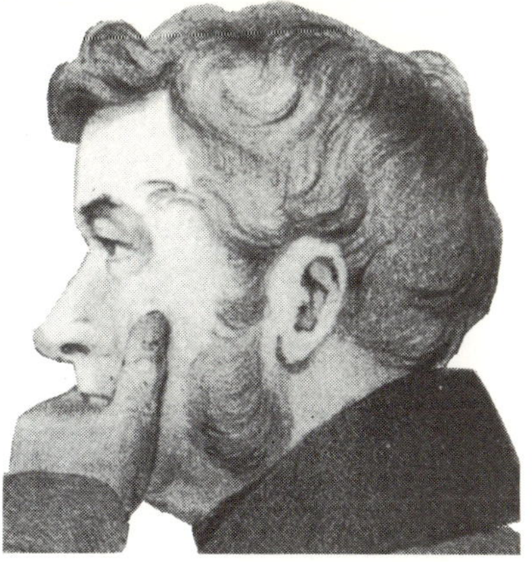

John Frost.

> Pontypool
> Sunday night, Nov 3rd, 1839
>
> Dear Parents, I hope this will find you well, as I am myself at this present. I shall this night be engaged in a glorious struggle for freedom, and should it please God to spare my life, I shall see you soon; but if not, grieve not for me. I shall have fallen in a noble cause. Farewell!
>
> Yours truly,
> George Shell (26)

The marchers in fact were overwhelmed, the leaders arrested, and some killed, including the lad who wrote the letter.

Feargus O'Connor the fiery speaker who inspired the Chartists.

Feargus O'Connor

In 1840 there were Chartist riots in several towns; some 500 leading Chartists were imprisoned. These included a fiery Irish orator who inspired the masses—Feargus O'Connor. In 1840 O'Connor had founded the National Charter Association, which was in fact the first attempt to set up a party for the working class. O'Connor had also started and edited a working-class newspaper, *The Northern Star*. The paper became the mouthpiece of the Chartist movement, sold well and was very influential. As O'Connor himself said: "the power of the press is acknowledged upon all hands, and rather than oppose it, I have preferred to arm myself with it."

O'Connor had a wide following, particularly in Yorkshire and Lancashire, and when he was released from prison in 1841, the hymn *The Lion of Freedom* was written in celebration.

> The lion of freedom comes from his den,
> We'll rally around him again and again.
> We'll crown with laurels our champion to be,
> O'Connor, the patriot of sweet liberty.
>
> The pride of the nation, he's noble and brave,
> He's the terror of tyrants, the friend of the slave.
> The bright star of freedom, the noblest of men,
> We'll rally around him again and again.

On facing page Cartoon depicting a physical force Chartist arming for the fight.

Though proud daring tyrants his body confined,
They never could alter his generous mind;
We'll hail our caged lion, now free from his den,
And we'll rally around him again and again.

Who strove for the patriots? Was up night and day?
And saved them from falling to tyrants and prey?
It was Feargus O'Connor was diligent then,
We'll rally around him again and again.

Physical Force Advocates

Some Chartist leaders could stir people up even more than O'Connor. An ex-Wesleyan Methodist Minister, Joseph Raynor Stephens, became an outspoken Chartist supporter. He spoke thus at Norwich: "I tell the rich to make their will. The people are with us, the soldiers are not against us. The working men have produced all the wealth and they are miserable . . . The working man is the ground landlord of all the property in the kingdom. If he has it not he has the right to come down on the rich until he gets it (27)."

Some Chartists began to arm themselves with muskets and

pikes, and small arsenals were collected. A section of the unemployed factory workers and colliers in the North seemed intent on a revolutionary class war. The Chartist movement was divided between advocates of physical force and those who supported moral force. Lovett, a champion of moral force, protested at the violence: "The whole physical force agitation is harmful and injurious to the movement. Muskets are not what are wanted, but education and schooling of the working people. Stephens and O'Connor are shattering the movement. Violent words do not slay the enemies but the friends of our movement (28)."

Moral Force

On occasions Lovett openly attacked O'Connor: "I regard Feargus O'Connor as . . . a man who, by his personal conduct, joined to his malignant influence in *The Northern Star*, has been the blight of democracy from the first moment he opened his lips as its professed advocate (29)."

The hostility between the two main Chartist leaders was mutual. O'Connor hated Lovett's support of moral force and education. Lovett had written a book entitled *Chartism, a new organization of the People*. The book stated the Chartist case and the need for education. It also provided rules and regulations for a proposed National Association of the United Kingdom for Promoting the Political and Social Improvement of the People. Certainly some Chartist schools developed, and even Chartist churches and Chartist abstinence societies. But O'Connor wrote scathingly of what he called "Knowledge Chartism," "Bible Chartism" and "Teetotal Chartism." He stated: "I object to Knowledge Chartism because it impliedly acknowledges a standard of some sort of learning, education, or information as a necessary qualification to entitle man to his political rights."

O'Connor was primarily concerned to prevent Chartism from being taken over by middle-class interests. As a rival to O'Connor's Association there emerged the Complete Suffrage Union led by Joseph Sturge, the Birmingham Quaker radical. The group was a combination of middle-class liberals, radicals and moral force Chartists. However, the complete Suffrage Union was never a real threat to O'Connor's dominance.

Religious Fervour

A religious fervour gripped some Chartists. Like the Primitive Methodists they held large open-air, or camp meetings, where prayers and hymns were sung. At one such meeting held on Clerkenwell Green in August 1840, the following prayer was offered for the imprisoned Chartists: "Oh most merciful Father! Whose Government, except where distorted by man, is all mercy! Remember, we entreat Thee, our brethren who are at this time confined in dark and gloomy dungeons, for endeavouring by peaceful and Scriptural means to obtain possession of just rights—visit them even there—strengthen them with the consolations of the Gospels, and though they are prevented from attending the public means of grace, support their minds; and if they should perish for want of the necessaries of life, receive their spirits, and may they dwell forever more with Thyself and the patriots that have gone before them . . . Thine eyes did follow the arrest—the trial—the effort to get convicted—yes the very verdict is recorded on high in Heaven's court . . . Hear our prayer for John Frost and his compatriots Williams and Jones, for Feargus O'Connor, for John Vincent, yea for the whole catalogue of patriots whose every case Thou art well acquainted with. Provide for their wives and families, may the children follow the steps of their fathers, as far as they have followed Thy holy example. We thank Thee for the past, we thank Thee for the future.

"Direct the Council of the people now sitting in a distant part of the country—may the means they may resort to be consistent with the glory, and further emancipation of Thy servants. Bless our enemies . . . and to Thy name, Oh Parent of mankind, shall be the glory, Amen (30)."

Chartists hymns were often sung to the accompaniment of rousing tunes. One such Chartist hymn went:

> See the brave, yet spirit broken,
> Who uphold your righteous cause;
> Who against them hath not spoken?
> They are, just as Jesus was,
> Persecuted
> By bad men and wicked laws.

> Rouse them from their silken slumbers,
> Trouble them amidst their pride;
> Swell your ranks, augment your numbers,
> Spread the Charter far and wide;
> Truth is with us,
> God himself is on our side.

The Second Petition

In 1842 a second Chartist petition, signed, it was claimed, by three million people, was presented to Parliament. The opening sentences were remarkably similar to the American Declaration of Independence and the French revolutionaries' Declaration of the Rights of Man: "Government originated from, was designed to protect the freedom and promote the happiness of, and ought to be responsible to, the whole people . . . Any form of Government which fails to effect the purposes for which it was designed . . . is unconstitutional, tyrannical, and ought to be amended or resisted."

The Petition listed the main working-class grievances as class legislation, heavy taxation, the new Poor Law, the disparity of wages and salaries, hours of work, and even church establishment. There was strong opposition to the Petition in the House

The procession attending the great national petition of 1842.

of Commons, particularly from Mr Macaulay, who said, "I believe that universal suffrage would be fatal to all purposes for which government exists, and that it is utterly incompatible with the very existence of civilization. I conceive that civilization rests on the security of property . . . You propose to give them supreme power; in every constituent body throughout the empire, capital and accumulated property is to be placed absolutely at the foot of labour . . . (31)."

The Plug Plot

The Petition was rejected by the House of Commons by 287 votes to 49. Strikes and riots followed, especially in Lancashire, where the so-called Plug Plot took place. Strikers marched from factory to factory, removing the boiler plugs in order to bring the steam engines to a standstill. Meetings of strikers began to pass resolutions that "all labour should cease until the People's Charter became the law of the land." The strikers were often starved back to work.

After 1842, however, there was some decline in the activitics of Chartists. Peel's programme of financial reform, a general improvement in trade, and railway building providing employment, were all contributory factors. The extent of Chartist activity certainly reflected the degree of economic hardship. One

A cartoon of 1843 showing Chartists presenting their petition to Parliament.

Chartist leader, Joseph Stephens, had always recognized the economic basis of Chartism: "The question of universal suffrage is a knife and fork question, a bread and meat question. If any man ask what I mean by universal suffrage, I mean to say that every working man in the land has a right to a good coat on his back, a good hat on his head, a good roof for the shelter of his household, a good dinner on his table, no more work than will keep him in health while at it, and as much wages as will keep him in the enjoyment of plenty, and all the blessings of life that reasonable men could desire."

O'Connor's Land Company

Yet as O'Connor said in 1844: "Chartism is not dead, but sleeping." In the following year he founded a land company to start Chartist settlements of smallholders. The plan was to "purchase land, erect dwellings and allot them to members upon such terms as shall enable them to become small freeholders, and to live in comparative comfort and independence." He addressed his fellow Chartists in these words: "You are, in a word, a poor, beggarly, lousy set of devils! Without house or home, or bread, or clothes, or fuel, begging the means of subsistence, and thankful to him who will coin your sweat into gold! Now mark what you might be—comfortable, independent, happy." Two such settlements were founded. O'Connorville and Charterville. By 1851 the ventures had ended in financial failure.

Meanwhile in 1845 O'Connor had given his journal a new title, *The Northern Star and National Trades Journal*, moved it from Leeds to London, and increased its price. O'Connor hoped that the new journal would "be the means of rallying the proper machinery for conducting the Land Movement, the National Trades' Movement, the Labour Movement, and the Charter Movement." O'Connor was to be disappointed. The trade unions, by and large, refused to have anything to do with Chartism—at least in its O'Connorite form.

In 1847 O'Connor was returned as MP for Nottingham. In this year trade again collapsed, and social and economic distress was acute by 1848. News came of widespread European revolts. In March 1848 the executive committee of the National Charter Association sent the following address to Paris. "Heroic Citi-

The Chartist meeting on Kennington Common.

zens [of Paris]. The thunder notes of your victory have sounded across the Channel, awakening the sympathies and hopes of every lover of liberty . . . By your courage . . . and devotion to principle, you have consecrated the sacred right of insurrection . . . The fire that consumed the throne of the royal traitor and tyrant will kindle the torch of liberty in every country in Europe."

The Third Petition

There were bread riots and other disturbances all over England, and a third Charter Petition was prepared. In substance it differed from those of 1839 and 1842, only in that O'Connor had dropped the demand for the ballot. It was arranged that on 10th April the Chartists would meet on Kennington Common, and then march with the Petition to Westminster. The Government took stiff precautions, enlisting troops and special constables, and placing the aged Duke of Wellington in charge. In the event, the crowd was much smaller than had been anticipated and was not allowed to cross the Thames. When the

Petition was examined it was found that of the boasted five million signatures, ". . . the number of signatures has been ascertained to be 1,975,496. It is further evident to your Committee that on numerous consecutive sheets the signatures are in one and the same handwriting. Your Committee also observed the names of distinguished individuals attached to the petition, who can scarcely be supposed to concur in its prayer: among which occurs the name of Her Majesty, as Victoria Rex, the Duke of Wellington, Sir Robert Peel etc, etc. Your Committee have also observed in derogation of the value of such petition, the insertion of numbers of names which are obviously fictitious, such as 'No Cheese,' 'Pug Nose,' 'Flat Nose.' There are others included, which your Committee do not hazard offending the House and the dignity and decency of their proceedings by reporting (32)."

The petition was rejected by 222 votes to 17. Chartism had become almost a laughing stock. Feargus O'Connor had to be removed from the House of Commons to a lunatic asylum in 1853, and he died two years later. However, he was not forgotten and 50,000 people went to his funeral.

Chartism lingered on for a further few years, but a change of character took place in 1850. The left-wing of the movement, headed first by Harney and later by Ernest Jones, took over the leadership of the National Charter Association. They remodelled Chartism as a socialist party, calling for the nationalization of the land, the mines and fisheries. A contemporary described the change thus: "Chartism in 1850 is a different thing from Chartism in 1840. The leaders of the English proletariat . . . have progressed from the idea of a simple, political reform to the idea of a social revolution (33)."

The Failure of Chartism

Why did Chartism fail? Clearly it was too ambitious; it lacked money and unity. The apathy of London was a serious disadvantage and the trade unions gave no official support. After 1848 wages rose and unemployment fell. The workers invested in friendly and co-operative societies, and looked to the trade unions to represent their grievances. Some Chartists, notably Lovett, had been all for wooing middle-class support, and certainly people like Sturge and Attwood had been ready to help.

However, Chartism never successfully linked up with the radical middle-class movements.

Did Chartism fail at all? Five of the Six points eventually became nationally accepted (abolition of property qualification—1858; vote by ballot—1872; payment of MPs—1911; adult male suffrage—1918; and equal electoral districts in successive stages as far as population movement has allowed). Chartism brought considerable attention to the conditions of the labouring classes, and marked a real step forward in the importance of working-class opinion. Once established, working-class movements were not only inevitable, they could no longer be ignored. As Harney prophesied in 1852; "Chartism itself will survive the wreck of parties and the ruin of politicians . . . its spirit has begun to exercise an influence over the country's politics; and all parties have come to acknowledge the potency of that democratic opinion (34)." The realization of Chartist and working-class demands had been only delayed.

William Lovett.

Robert Owen — champion of the Co-operative Movement.

3 *Co-operation and Co-operators*

AS EARLY AS 1760, there had been co-operative corn mills at Chatham and Woolwich where groups of workmen had joined together to run their own mills. Weavers at Fenwick had opened a co-operative store in 1769. But these early efforts by associations of men to provide one another with work did not last long.

Robert Owen

We usually think of Robert Owen not only as the founder of the Co-operative Movement, but also as the father of British socialism. He was a self-made man and a model employer at his New Lanark mills. Between 1813 and 1816 he wrote four essays entitled *A New View of Society* in which he stated the belief that: "Man's character is made for him and not by him," and he went on in other writings to state "that manual labour, properly directed, is the source of all wealth and of national prosperity." He believed that men should work to produce happiness not profits; that "to buy cheap and sell dear" would hurt and perhaps destroy "man's finest and best faculties." Owen's idea was to set up villages or communities of co-operation in which to try out these views.

Owen's writings bore fruit in 1821. In London, he established the Co-operative and Economical Society, with William Lovett (the future Chartist leader) as storekeeper. Similar co-operative trading societies were formed throughout the country. Lovett himself described them thus: "The members subscribed a small weekly sum for the raising of a common fund, with which they opened a general store, containing such articles of food, clothing, books etc, as were most in request among workmen; the profits of which were added to the common stock. As their fund increased some of them employed their members; such as shoemakers, tailors, and other domestic trades, paying them journeymen's wages, and adding the profits to their funds. Many of them were also enabled by these means to raise sufficient capital to commence manufacture on a small scale; such as broadcloth, silk, linen, worsted goods, shoes, hats, cutlery, furniture, etc (35)."

Dr King

In 1828 a Dr William King founded some co-operative associations and the *Co-operator* newspaper at Brighton. This is how King himself described the venture: "A number of persons, chiefly of the working class, having read several works on the subject of co-operation, conceived the possibility of reducing it to practice in some shape or other. They accordingly formed themselves into a society; and met once a week for reading and conversation on the subject; they also began a weekly subscription of 1d. The members who joined were considerable—at one time upwards of 170; but, as happens in such cases, many were lukewarm and indifferent, and the numbers fluctuated. Those who remained began at once an evident improvement in their minds. When the subscription amounted to £5, it was invested in groceries, which were retailed to the members. Business kept increasing. The first week the amount sold was half-a-crown [12½p]; it is now about £38. The profit is about 10 per cent; so that a return of £20 a week pays all expenses, besides which the members have a large room to meet in and work in. About six months ago, the society took a lease of 28 acres of land, about nine miles from Brighton, which they cultivate as garden and nursery out of their surplus capital. They employ on the garden, out of 75 members, four and sometimes five men, with their own capital (36)."

Dr William King — founder of the *Co-operator* newspaper.

The *Co-operator* urged the adoption of the Brighton model in manufacturing as well: "when the capital has accumulated sufficiently the Society may produce any manufactures they please, and so provide for all their wants of food, clothing and houses."

By 1830 there were about three hundred co-operative societies in the country, although many were short-lived. Owen established a co-operative community at Orbiston near Glasgow in 1825, and a similar venture at Queenwood in Hampshire in 1839. These soon ran into difficulties and did not survive long.

Owen had also organized what he called labour exchanges, or bazaars. In these exchanges, materials and commodities could be exchanged for other goods or for labour notes in terms of the number of hours of labour needed to produce them. At first they were popular and successful, but administrative difficulties inevitably arose.

Wholesale Venture

In 1831 a Co-operative Congress, held in Manchester, founded the North and West of England United Co-operative Company which established a wholesale warehouse in Liverpool to serve all the societies and to help in the exchange of goods they produced. Its purpose was "to unite all the societies in this part of the kingdom into one body, for mutual protection and advantage, and for the interchange of kind offices and benevolent actions." The 1833 Congress asserted the independence of the Co-operative Movement from Owen's well-known

Robert Owen's settlement at Orbiston.

A labour note printed for Robert Owen's Equitable Labour Exchange (1833).

atheist and socialist views. It carried a resolution "that co-operators as such are not pledged to any political, religious or irreligious tenets whatsoever; neither those of Mr Owen nor of any other individual." William Lovett actually attributed the failure of many of the early co-operative ventures in the 1830s to religious differences: "The question of religion was not productive of much dissention (sic) until Mr Owen's return from America when his 'Sunday Morning Lectures' excited the alarm of the religious portion of his members, and caused great numbers to secede (37)."

Opposition to Owen's Ideas

Moreover, there was opposition to Robert Owen's influence in other spheres. The *Poor Man's Guardian* spoke for many working-class leaders when it discussed Owen's land schemes: "The Owenite thinks that without property, the working classes can never get represented in Parliament, and therefore he sets to work with his 'Equitable Labour Exchange' to get property; while the Radical thinks that without representation they will never be able to acquire property at all, and accordingly he begins to work at the other end, and goes to work for Universal Suffrage . . . No one can admire Mr Owen more than we do, nor entertain a higher opinion of his enlightened views; but, at the same time, we are of the opinion that if he supposes that the wealth-producers of England will ever reap the fruits of his benevolence, until they shall have first obtained their political rights, he greatly deceives himself, and will find it so, when it is too late (38)."

The Owenite movement then was seen by some as elitist, with middle-class leadership. Friedrich Engels, a friend of Karl Marx and a contemporary observer, discounted the Owenites' contribution to the wider Labour Movement. He made some interesting comments on their social origins: "They are recruited in part from the working class of which they have enlisted but a very small fraction, representing, however, its most educated and solid elements . . . They acknowledged no historical development and wish to place this nation in a state of Communism at once, overnight, not by the unavoidable march of its political development up to the point at which this transition becomes both possible and necessary (39)."

The "Dividend"

It is perhaps worth noting that the idea of a "dividend" was introduced by several of the early co-operative societies, as the following extract of a report by a London co-operative society in 1832, indicates: "An interesting discussion ensued upon the propriety of altering the laws [of the Society] so as to allow a percentage to every member in proportion to the amount of his dealings. The members appeared to be generally of the opinion that the adoption of the proposition would be a considerable advantage, as it would confer immediate benefit upon all those who dealt extensively at the store, and remove the discouragements which the most zealous and persevering Co-operators had hitherto experienced . . .

"It was moved, seconded, and carried by a large majority: that every member of the Union shall receive a percentage upon his dealings, to be paid quarterly."

Many of the early Owenite co-operative societies died out in the late 1830s (although some thirty-seven of them were still in existence in 1890, and twenty-seven survived until 1914). By the 1840s the Co-operative Movement needed new strength, almost a new beginning.

The Rochdale Pioneers

The Rochdale Pioneers provided this fresh start. They opened a store in Toad Lane, Rochdale, in 1844. There had been earlier attempts at co-operation in Rochdale in the 1830s, but in 1844 some twenty-eight weavers invested £1 each in setting up the Rochdale Society of Equitable Pioneers and declared: "The objects and plans of this Society are to form arrangements for the pecuniary benefit and the improvement of the social and domestic condition of its members, by raising a sufficient amount of capital in shares of one pound each, to bring into operation the following places and arrangements:

"The establishment of a Store for the sale of provisions, clothing, etc.

"The building, purchasing, or erecting a number of houses, in which those members, desiring to assist each other in improving their domestic and social conditions, may reside.

"To commence the manufacture of such articles as the society may determine upon, for the employment of such members as may be without employment, or who may be suffering in consequence of repeated reductions in their wages.

Thirteen of the original members of the Rochdale Society of Equitable Pioneers.

The first co-operative shop, opened in Rochdale in 1844.

"As a further benefit and security to the members of this Society, the Society shall purchase or rent an estate or estates of land, which shall be cultivated by the members who may be out of employment, or whose labour may be badly remunerated . . .

"That, for the promotion of sobriety, a Temperance Hotel be opened in one of the Society's houses as soon as convenient (40)."

Educational Activities

This last aim was obviously an indication of the teetotal views of some of the Pioneers, many of whom were Methodists. There was a dispute between these Methodist Pioneers and those who were Owenite socialists over the holding of lectures and discussion meetings on Sundays. The Sabbatarian Methodists, who were very much against the idea, lost the argument, and the educational work of the Society on Sundays and weekdays flourished. In 1857 the Society decided to devote $2\frac{1}{2}$ per cent of the profits for educational purposes, for example, the maintenance of a newsroom and library, and the running of education classes. This decision, like so many that the Pioneers took, was of historical importance. Many other co-operative societies, modelling themselves on the Rochdale pattern, adopted the $2\frac{1}{2}$ per cent educational principle. The Rochdale Pioneers then, saw themselves essentially as a working-class movement, with a

Charles Kingsley.

E V Neale.

democratic basis, one man one vote. Interest was paid on the share capital invested by members, and after providing for educational purposes any profit was to be distributed as a dividend on purchases made by members.

The Christian Socialists

In 1848 a number of clergymen and lawyers formed a national group, calling themselves the Christian Socialists. They gave money and advice to working-class movements generally. The leaders included F D Maurice, a clergyman and professor, Charles Kingsley and Thomas Hughes, both well-known authors, and J M Ludlow and E V Neale, both lawyers. In particular the Christian Socialists sponsored co-operative workshops, run by the workers themselves. The workers were to choose their own chairman, secretary, treasurer and council of administration, and profits were to be shared amongst themselves. However, there was little initiative from the workers and, on the whole, the experiment was a failure.

Meanwhile in 1850, the Rochdale Society opened a Wholesale Department for the use of other co-operative societies in the area. In the same year it took over a corn mill which eventually provided for the needs of retail societies throughout Lancashire. The objects of the mill were "to manufacture flour and meal free from adulteration, and . . . to divide the profits amongst members in proportion to their trade with the Society." In 1854 the Rochdale Manufacturing Company

On facing page Meeting of the Manchester and Salford Co-operative Society in 1865.

was set up, undertaking both the spinning and weaving of cotton. The Rochdale model, then, provided for producers' as well as consumers' co-operation, and for wholesale as well as retail trade. But the Pioneers never ventured into the Owenite ideals of co-operative communities; they were practical, level-headed men, and they worked for, and achieved profits. As the *Co-operator* in the 1860s put it: "The present co-operative movement does not seek to level the social inequalities which exist in society as regards wealth, but only to lessen the exploitation of the workman . . . Modern Co-operation means a union of working men for the improvement of the social circumstances of the class to which they belong . . . it is the working man's lever, by which he may rise in the world."

Co-operative retail societies based on the Rochdale model spread quickly. By 1860 there were some 400 and by the late 1860s there were over a thousand, with a total membership of half a million. Letters to the *Co-operator* stated the case for a national wholesale society. One William Bond, secretary of the Reading Industrial Co-operative Society, wrote in January

Wholesale Co-operation

1861: "Let a Wholesale Co-operative Society be organized by all the Stores at present in existence, and let the shares be, say £20 each; then each Store could subscribe for one, two or more shares towards the capital, up to as many shares as it may be thought fit to limit it. The Society could be worked by a committee chosen at the annual conference from the various representatives of the Stores, in the same way as for an ordinary store, and participating in the profits upon the same principle. By this means all the lesser stores would be enabled to obtain goods as pure and as cheap as those who have the largest capital."

In 1864 the North of England Co-operative Wholesale Society was set up, which was owned by the local consumers' societies. In 1872 the North of England part was dropped, and the CWS, as it became known, was soon a national organization, and made rapid advances. It manufactured its own goods by opening several factories. In 1871 the *Co-operative News*, printed by the Co-operative Printing Society, began a long and influential career. It immediately pressed for co-operative manufactures: "At last, some of our enthusiastic correspondents will say, at last a new step in Co-operative progress is about to be realized, by the commencement of manufacturing processes on behalf of the whole of the federated stores. Our more timid friends, who have listened from time to time to orations by the leaders of society, in which co-operation has been gently patted on the back as a very good thing for working people so long as it is kept to the work of distribution, will hold their breath at the announcement that the representatives of 264 stores have resolved to try to produce some of the various goods which they keep in stock (41)."

By 1914 co-operative goods valued at more than £9 million were being produced by 20,000 workers. The Co-operative Movement had become vast, and was in danger of losing its ideals. Many of the idealists in the movement found satisfaction in educational work. Professor Stuart, the pioneer of university extension classes, speaking to the Co-operative Congress in 1879 said: "Your movement is a democratic one if ever there was one . . . first you must educate your members in your own principles and in those of economic science . . . and in the sec-

Arnold Toynbee, the English political economist and social reformer.

ond place you must educate them generally. Education is desirable for all mankind; it is the life's necessity for co-operators."

Co-operative Education

Many co-operative societies had followed the Rochdale model in organizing classes in scientific, technical, art, commercial and general subjects. These early co-operative classes were successful because in the middle of the nineteenth century there were few alternative sources of education for the working classes. At the 1882 Co-operative Congress Arnold Toynbee, a great social worker, read a paper on co-operative education. In this paper he pointed out that elementary education was being provided by the State, and higher education by the universities, and he asked: "what part of education then is left for co-operators to appropriate? The answer that I would give is the education of the citizen." Certainly the democratic organization of the Co-operative Movement, with the local monthly members' meetings and democratic elections of management committees, provided excellent opportunities for a training in citizenship. Towards the end of the nineteenth century the Co-operative Movement concentrated more on strictly co-operative education. For example, classes were held in co-operative book-keeping and auditing and co-operative management. Outlines of lessons were published and correspondence courses organized.

The Women's Guild

The Women's Co-operative Guild was established in 1883, and again one of the first branches was at Rochdale. By 1910 there were 521 branches with a membership of nearly 26,000. The Guild encouraged its members not only to take a full and active part in the Co-operative Movement, but also in the social and political life of the community as a whole. While membership was open to all, in practice the majority of its members were working class. The local guilds did much to help the general education of women, and play a part in their emancipation.

The *Co-operative News* carried a Women's Corner, and the first article in 1883 read: "We can be independent members of our Store, but we are only asked to come and buy . . . why should not we women do more than we do? Surely, without departing from our own sphere, and without trying to undertake work which can be better done by men, there is more for us women to do than spend money. Spend our money at our own Store we must, that is a matter of course; but our duty does not end here, nor our duty to our fellow creatures. To come and 'buy' is all we can be asked to do; but cannot we go further ourselves? Why should not we have our meetings, our readings, our discussions? (42)"

The Co-operative Party

At the 1897 Co-operative Congress a resolution was passed calling for direct co-operative representation in Parliament. Some delegates protested "no politics in co-operation," but the chairman responded: "I do not seek to introduce politics into Co-operation, but to see more Co-operation introduced into politics." But scarcely any of the societies were prepared to devote any money to support parliamentary candidates. Not until 1917 did the movement found its own Co-operative Party. This was officially separate from the Labour Party, but worked in close harmony with it, and co-operative funds went to secure the election of some Labour MPs.

By the twentieth century the Co-operative Movement had many successes to its credit, but as the Report of the Royal Commission on the Poor Laws in 1909 noted: "The chief success of Co-operation has been among the artisan class—not to any considerable extent either among the poorest classes or the better off."

As a self-help, democratic working-class movement, the Co-operative Movement clearly played a major role within the total Labour Movement. It helped large numbers of people, not only in economic, but in social and educational terms.

4 Unions and Unionists

An early trade union banner.

THE EARLY TRADE UNIONS were mostly local trade clubs. Membership of them was largely restricted to skilled craftsmen. The subscriptions were generally too high for the poorly paid unskilled labourers. Many of these clubs provided sickness benefits and funeral expenses. Often they were indistinguishable from friendly societies. Here is an example:

Friendly Societies

"Benefit Society of Journeymen Shoemakers instituted in the year 1780.

"Subscription: Entrance 2s 6d [2 shillings and 6 pence or 12½p]. Monthly payment 1s 3d [6p]. When the stock is under £20 the box to be declared shut; and 1d per week extra to be paid to support the sick; and 1s [5p] by each member on half-yearly night.

"Benefits: Sick: To the sick, when stock is above £20, 7s [35p] per week; when under £20, 4s [20p] per week.

"Superannuated: A member, after being 6 months on the box, to be declared superannuated and to receive 4s per week for 6 months more. After that, if unable to work, to receive 2s 6d per week for life or till recovered.

"Death: A member's funeral £7, his wife's £5."

It was natural that such trade clubs should be a place for discussion on questions of wages and conditions, and that they should consider the possibility of action when wage rates were threatened. There was sometimes an attempt to co-ordinate action over a wider area by forming workers' combinations.

Membership card (left) and articles of the Society of Journeymen Brushmakers.

THE

UNITED SOCIETY

OF

JOURNEYMEN

BRUSH MAKERS.

RECEIVER'S BLANK.

London:

PRINTED FOR THE SOCIETY BY

J. R. LARKIN, 6, NORTHAMPTON SQUARE.

MDCCCLI.

ARTICLES

OF

THE SOCIETY

OF

JOURNEYMEN BRUSH-MAKERS,

HELD AT THE

SIGN OF THE CRAVEN HEAD,

DRURY LANE.

LONDON:

INSTITUTED IN THE YEAR

1806.

Knight and Compton, Printers, Middle Street, Cloth Fair

The Combination Acts

As the terror in France increased, the ruling classes in Britain became increasingly nervous that revolution might break out among British workers. A mutiny in the navy at the Nore in 1797, and a rising in Ireland in 1798 increased the fears of the Government. In 1799 and 1800 Parliament took action to suppress combinations of workers by passing the Combination Acts. The 1799 Act made such combinations illegal and the 1800 Act added such clauses as, "all contracts, covenants, and agreements whatsoever . . . heretofore made . . . between any journeymen manufacturers or other persons . . . for obtaining an advance of wages of them or any of them . . . or for lessening or altering any of their usual hours or time of working, or for decreasing the quantity of work . . . or for preventing or hindering any person or persons from employing whomsoever he, she, or they shall think proper to employ shall be illegal, null and void . . . No journeyman, workman, or other person shall at any time after the passing of this Act make or enter into . . . any such contract, covenant or agreement . . ."

In spite of these Acts combinations continued to exist, disguised as friendly societies, which were not affected by the legislation. But in general it may be said that in the early nineteenth century, British workers were almost entirely at the mercy of the magistrates and employers. No wonder that the Luddite Riots and other disturbances took place.

Friendly societies concentrated on social and medical benefits. They were often founded on some ethical or religious basis, but excluding politics, and made rapid increases in membership. The attitude of the middle and upper classes towards friendly societies was understandably one of suspicion. But eventually such societies became respected and admired as successful self-help working-class movements.

However, at the beginning of the nineteenth century workers joining or forming trade clubs or combinations were heavily penalized. The *Manchester Observer* of 30th January, 1819 reported: "Pilkington and Kay, weavers of Bury, have been sentenced to two years' imprisonment in Lancaster Castle for conspiracy to raise wages. Several spinners have also been sent to Lancaster Castle for two years, for a similar offence."

Francis Place, from a portrait by S Drummond.

Repeal of the Combination Laws

By the 1820s outbreaks of violence and rioting had died out. Francis Place, a London tailor, and Joseph Hume, a radical MP, worked together successfully to bring about the repeal of the Combination Laws in 1824. At once secret societies, which were really trade unions, came out into the open, causing an outbreak of strikes. The Government was seriously alarmed and passed the Amendment Act of 1825. This Act, while legalizing combinations for dealing with questions of wages and hours, imposed penalties against what it termed "intimidation, molestation or obstruction" and against any attempt "to coerce" either employers or employees. In other words the trade unions were limited to peaceful bargaining.

The Amendment Act

These early unions included the Steam Engine Makers' (1825); the Northumberland and Durham Colliers' Union (1825); the Carpenters and Joiners' (1827); the Potters' (1831); and the Builders' (1831). In 1829 John Doherty had organized the Grand General Union of All the Operative Spinners of the United Kingdom, the first national union to be attempted. In 1830 he launched the National Association for the Protection of Labour, and invited every trade society in the country to join. The funds of the Association "shall be applied only to prevent reductions of wages, but in no case to procure an advance. Any

The First National Union

trade considering their wages too low may exert themselves to obtain such an advance, as they may think necessary and can obtain it by their own exertions (43)." (A more moderate approach by today's standards would be hard to imagine!) By 1831 the combined membership of the Association was 100,000, but the union never really prospered. Each trade or section was only interested in its own interests and conflicts.

Robert Owen and Unionism

What Doherty had failed to achieve Robert Owen set his hand to. In October 1833 he put forward the idea of a general union of the productive classes. As a result of a conference called in February 1834, he set up the Grand National Consolidated Trades Union. This was to be open to all the workers in the country. Unfortunately none of the four major unions—builders, potters, spinners and clothiers agreed to join. Owen saw his union as a means of creating the new type of society that he desired. "That although the design of the Union is, in the first instance, to raise the wages of the workmen, or prevent any further reduction therein, and to diminish the hours of labour, the great and ultimate object of it must be to establish the paramount rights of Industry and Humanity . . . consequently the Unionists should lose no opportunity of mutually encouraging and assisting each other in bringing about A DIFFERENT ORDER OF THINGS, in which the really useful and intelligent part of society only shall have the direction of affairs, and in which a well-directed industry and virtue shall meet their just distinction and reward, and vicious idleness its well-merited contempt and destitution."

The workers responded enthusiastically to Owen's ideas. Within a few weeks farm workers, miners, tailors, gas workers, bakers and others had joined, bringing the membership to about half a million. However, there was no strong control over the union. Instead of building up strike funds, some of the local branches squandered their resources. "After paying entrance fees our society had about forty pounds to spare, and not knowing what better to do with it we engaged Mr Thomas Jones to paint for us a banner, at a cost of twenty-five pounds. We also purchased a full set of secret order regalia, surplices, trimmed aprons, etc, and a crown and robes (44)."

The Tolpuddle Martyrs, from an oil painting by Gilbert Spencer.

The Tolpuddle Martyrs

Robert Owen's giant union lasted six months. Employers hated and feared the Grand National. The first blow came in March 1834. Six Dorsetshire farm labourers, the Tolpuddle Martyrs as they became known, were transported for seven years. Their offence was that they allegedly took an illegal oath at a local ceremony when joining the GNCTU. The report of the trial brought sympathy for the labourers, but was a setback for the union.

"John Lock—We all went into Thomas Stanfield's house into a room upstairs . . . One of the men asked if we were ready. We said, yes. One of them said, 'Then bind your eyes' and we took out handkerchiefs and bound over our eyes. They then led us into another room on the same floor. Someone then read a paper, but I don't know what the meaning was. After that we were asked to kneel down, which we did. Then there was some more reading: I don't know what it was about. It seemed to be out of some part of the Bible. Then we got up and took off the bandages from our eyes. I had then seen James Lovelace and John Stanfield in the room. Someone read again, but I don't know what it was, and then we were told to kiss the book, when our eyes were unblinded, and I saw the book which looked like a little Bible . . . They said we were as brothers: that when we were to stop for wages we should not tell our masters ourselves, but that the masters would have a note or a letter sent to them (45)."

George Loveless, the leader of the Martys, was a Wesleyan Methodist local preacher. While he was in gaol, awaiting transportation, he wrote this verse:

God is our Guide! From field, from wave,
From plough, from anvil and from loom,
We come, our country's rights to save,
And speak the tyrant faction's doom;
We raise the watchword Liberty—
We will, we will, we will be free.

Many demonstrations were held to protest at the cruel treatment of the Tolpuddle Martyrs. So great was the public sympathy aroused that after four years they were freed.

The Document

Some employers, in an effort to destroy the GNCTU, forced their employees to sign what was termed the "Document": "We, the undersigned . . . do hereby declare that we are not in any way connected with the Union . . . and that we do not and will not contribute to the support of such members of the said union as are or may be out of work, in consequence of belonging to such union."

A contemporary artist's impression of four of the Tolpuddle Martyrs.

CONVICTED OF FELONY,
And Transported for SEVEN YEARS.

COUNTY OF DORSET,
Dorchester Division.
February 22d. 1834.

C. B. WOLLASTON,
JAMES FRAMPTON,
WILLIAM ENGLAND,
THOS. DADE,
JNO. MORTON COLSON,

HENRY FRAMPTON,
RICHD. TUCKER STEWARD,
WILLIAM R. CHURCHILL,
AUGUSTUS FOSTER.

G. CLARK, PRINTER, CORNHILL, DORCHESTER.

THE MEN CONCERNED

The employers used the lock-out as their first weapon. They closed their factories and yards to all workers until they signed the Document. This in turn led to strikes, but the men were forced to give in through lack of funds. By August 1834 it had become evident that the Grand National was breaking up, and Owen announced its dissolution.

The four big unions of the potters, spinners, builders and clothiers, although not officially linked with the GNCTU, were adversely affected by its fall. Trade unionism lived on in a local context, and improving trade after 1842 led to the founding or revival of national unions. For example, the coal miners, cotton spinners, printers, potters, glassmakers, tailors, shoemakers and others all formed national unions. In 1844 the Miners' Association began a long and bitter strike to improve wages and conditions. The mine owners brought in non-union men, largely Welsh and Irish, in an effort to break the solidarity of the miners. Many local Primitive Methodist ministers supported the strikers. As a writer of the time said of the strike: "Prayers for its success were offered up in the chapels; it was no uncommon thing for a wayside crowd to join in supplicating the assistance of Heaven, and to request that the men who were brought from a distance to work in a colliery—the 'black-legs' as they called them—might be injured." The strike was defeated, but the Association continued for another three years before it came to an end in the 1847–48 trade slump.

New Model Unionism

The position of trade unionism around 1850 was bleak, but far from hopeless. What was needed was a new breakthrough. The Amalgamated Society of Engineers (ASE) was formed in 1851, by an amalgamation of several smaller societies with the Steam Engine Makers. The ASE has been termed the "new model" as several amalgamated societies or unions modelled themselves on the ASE in the next ten to twenty years. The ASE placed great emphasis on the payment of benefits. To pay for these benefits a high subscription was necessary. William Allan was appointed as a full-time general secretary. The Society was particularly opposed to overtime working. "That in order to secure to our members a good general prospect of employment, we repudiate 'systematic overtime' as being the cause of much evil, through giving to a number the privilege of working more than a legitimate week's time, whilst doing so deprives other members of situations, producing much domestic misery and causing a great expenditure of the Society's funds (46)."

In 1852 the ASE refused to work systematic overtime. In return the employers, particularly in Lancashire and London, declared a general lock-out of all ASE members. The struggle lasted for three months. The ASE received sympathy and financial support from other unions, the Christian Socialists and from the general public. *The Times*, however, came out on the side of the employers. "We state in plain language why the masters cannot give way. They cannot do so because by such an act they would forfeit the indispensable rights of employers to make their own terms for labour in an open market . . . The men should yield because their objects are absolutely impracticable, and wholly inconsistent with the natural laws of society (47)."

A membership certificate of the General Union of House Carpenters and Joiners, founded 1860

Robert Applegarth.

George Potter.

In the end the engineers were forced back to work, but their union was not weakened by the struggle. Membership of the ASE doubled over the next ten years. In conscious imitation of the engineers, the Amalgamated Society of Carpenters and Joiners, with Robert Applegarth as Secretary; the Bricklayers, with Edwin Coulson as Secretary; and the Tailors and Plasterers were all formed in the next few years. Some other unions like the Ironfounders, with Daniel Guile as Secretary, modified their constitutions and policies to conform with the new model.

The Junta

These new general secretaries, with their central offices in London, often met in what was termed the "Clique" and later the "Junta." They became the leading spirits in the London Trades Council, formed in 1860. On the whole, the Council preferred a moderate policy. However one general secretary, George Potter of the Builders, was a militant trade unionist and editor of the one really effective working-class newspaper the *Beehive*. In 1867 Potter organized a national trade union conference, which was shunned by the Junta and their unions. But the conference was a success and was followed by the first meeting of the Trades Union Congress in 1868. By 1871 the Junta had accepted the TUC as the central authority of the trade union movement.

The Mechanics' Institute where the first Trades Union Congress was held in 1868.

The Sheffield Outrages

Meanwhile the very existence of the trade union movement had been threatened in 1866. The house of a Sheffield saw-grinder, who had refused to join a trade union, was wrecked by a can of gunpowder thrown down the chimney. In 1867 a Royal Commission was set up "to enquire and report on the organization and rules of trades' and other associations, with power to investigate any secret acts of intimidation, outrage or wrong alleged to have been promoted, encouraged, or connived at . . ."

Robert Applegarth welcomed the examination. "If a searching investigation leads to the discovery of an ulcer in our system, however small it may be, let the knife go to the very core," he said. The Commission Report made some interesting discoveries. "The first subject which engaged our attention was that of 'rattening.' Rattening is a mode of enforcing payment of contributions to and compliance with the rules of the Union. The wheel-bands, tool and other materials of a workman, are taken and held in pledge until he has satisfied the society by payment of his arrears, or by submitting to the rules which he has infringed. At first it was denied that the unions connived at this practice, but we had not proceeded far with our investigation before it was admitted on all hands that rattening had been prevalent for a long time in the grinding trades . . .

"The practice of rattening is well known to be illegal, and persons detected in illegally taking away property have frequently been convicted and punished. The excuse offered by the unions for this system is, that in the absence of legal powers, rattening affords the most ready means of enforcing payment of contributions and obedience to the rules of the union . . .

"The system of rattening has generally proved successful in effecting its object. If, however, the person rattened continues refractory, he commonly receives an anonymous letter warning him on the consequences of his obstinacy. If this warning is disregarded, recourse has been had to acts of outrage, the nature of which will be understood from a perusal of the cases actually investigated by us (48)."

Hornby v Close

Whilst these investigations were proceeding, a second blow befell the unions, known as the "Hornby v Close" case. The Society of Boilermakers prosecuted the treasurer of its Bradford branch for withholding society funds. But the judge who heard the case ruled that trade unions could not bring a case at law against any of their officers. This meant that trade union funds were virtually at the mercy of any dishonest official.

The findings of the Royal Commission now took on a new urgency. Trade unionists had to justify their existence before the Commission, and obtain an amendment of the law which would

Thomas Hughes, a Christian Socialist and writer of the book *Tom Brown's Schooldays.*

ensure their legality and protect their funds. The trade unions were fortunate in having two sympathizers on the Commission, Thomas Hughes and Frederic Harrison, both lawyers and Christian Socialists.

The Royal Commission

The enquiry lasted two years, and the Commissioners issued their Report in March 1869. The Sheffield Outrages were shown to be the work of a very small minority. The main body of the Report tried to justify the existence of trade unions and their legal protection, but picketing was condemned. "With regard to the right of workmen to combine together for determining and stipulating with their employer the terms on which only they will consent to work for him, we think that, provided the combination be perfectly voluntary, and that full liberty be left to all other workmen to undertake the work which the parties combining have refused, and that no obstruction be placed in the way of the employer resorting elsewhere in search of a supply of labour, there is no ground of justice or of policy for withholding such a right from the workmen . . .

"So far as relates to members of the union, promoting the strike, the pickets cannot be necessary if the members are voluntarily concurring therein; so far as relates to workmen who are not members of the union, picketing implies in principle an interference with their right to dispose of their labour as they think fit, and is, therefore, without justification; and so far as relates to the employer, it is a violation of his right of free resort to the labour market for the supply of such labour as he requires (79)."

Trade Union Legislation

Gladstone's Liberal Government acted on the recommendations of the Commissioners. The Trade Union Act of 1871 gave the unions legal status and protection. But a second Act, the Criminal Law Amendment Act, made picketing illegal. This was a sad blow to the unions. They regarded picketing as an essential weapon of a successful strike. However, when Disraeli and the Conservatives were returned at the 1874 General Election, the Criminal Law Amendment Act was repealed and replaced by the Conspiracy and Protection of Property Act of 1875. The Act legalized peaceful picketing. This was a considerable concession to the trade unions and a great gain for them.

Alexander MacDonald, a miners' leader who was one of the first trade union MPs.

The Miners

Meanwhile unionism had been gaining footholds amongst labouring groups. The miners had formed the National Association in 1863 under the leadership of Alexander MacDonald. The Association continued to survive, despite a split in 1869. MacDonald, who became an MP in 1874, preferred peaceful persuasion to strikes. He also pressed for co-operative collieries as a means of dividing wealth equally. The following is an account of MacDonald's speech at the 1875 national conference of miners:

"He [Mr A MacDonald] did not want to take one half-dollar or one half-cent from any man who had acquired his money fairly; but the present relation was that the few went riding in wealth, while the many were born to overwhelming poverty [cheers]. They had amended the laws—or, at any rate, the laws had been amended to some extent [hear, hear]. They must amend the social relations of the working classes still further [cheers]. The land was passing, and had been for years, from the hands of the old aristocracy and men who gained it by stealth and violence [cheers]. Vast accumulations had passed into the hands of a very few. He did not say it had been stolen from labour, but it had passed into other hands, from the folly and ignorance of the masses [hear, hear]. Their object must be to teach these masses, and when they taught them, to let others understand the meaning of their teaching—that by every legal means they should do what they could to have a more equal division of that which is the product of capital and labour—a more equal division between employer and employed [cheers]. The true way to this end was by co-operative collieries and institutions everywhere . . . (50)."

The Miners' National Association suffered during the years of the economic depression of the late 1870s and after MacDonald's death in 1881 it ceased to be influential at national level. The fall in the price of coal worked to the disadvantage of the miners because of the "sliding scale" method of payment. Under the sliding scale, wages would vary upwards or downwards according to the rise or fall in the selling price of coal. Local unions pressed hard for the introduction of a set minimum wage. In 1888 a national conference of local unions pledged to abolish the sliding scale and founded the Miners' Federation of Great Britain. By 1893 it had over 200,000 members and most districts had abolished the sliding scale system. The membership of the Federation continued to grow, reaching 600,000 by 1908 and 900,000 by 1920.

Joseph Arch and the Agricultural Labourers

The agricultural labourers at last founded a union in 1872. It was led by Joseph Arch, himself a farm labourer and a keen Primitive Methodist preacher in Warwickshire. The Union gained strength rapidly despite opposition from farmers, gentry

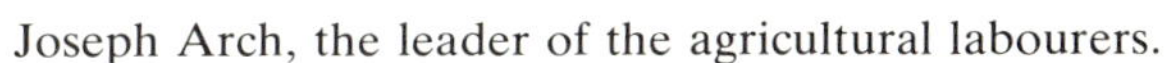

Joseph Arch, the leader of the agricultural labourers.

and parsons. The union campaigned for a minimum wage of 16s (80p) a week for labourers, and £1 for wagoners, a working day of $9\frac{1}{2}$ hours, and a vote for agricultural labourers. In an atmosphere of falling agricultural prices, farmers had to keep their production costs low, and so resisted the unionists. The song that follows is typical of others written in the 1870s to lift the morale of agricultural labourers and unionists:

Oh Dear! What'll Become of us?

Tune—Oh Dear! What Can the Matter Be?

What's a labourer's prospect in this land of freedom?
Six young uns to keep, and twelve shillings to feed 'em.
A jail and a workhouse, for all those who need 'em;
Pray what does a labourer lack?

Chorus: Oh dear! what'll become of us?
Oh dear! what'll become of us?
Oh dear! what'll become of us?
If he should give us the sack.

Twelve shillings a week, it'll just fill one belly;
But Bill, Tom and Hal, Polly, Susan, and Nelly,
They eat all day long, my old woman'll tell ye;
I only can just get a snack.

Oh dear! etc.

There came an old chap, whom the Union engages,
To show the poor man how to go for more wages;
Says he, "Ask for more, and if Farmer Grumps rages,
The Union will stand at your back."

Oh dear! etc.

Says Grumps, "If you join, it will end in disaster;
How dare you offend such an excellent master?"
Says I, "If you say so, we'll join all the faster."
Oh, he looked awfully black!

Oh dear! etc.

Joseph Arch addressing agricultural workers. Some of them have climbed into the tree to hear him more clearly.

He says, "In the harvest we're putting him quite about,"
Yet, if he'd be just, there'd be nothing to fight about;
But he swears he'll send us all to the right about,
When he begins to get slack.

Oh dear! etc.

There's plenty of work to be had by the willing.
With wages at double the paltry twelve shilling.
And land o'er the sea, to be had for the tilling,
If he should tell us to pack.

Oh dear! etc.

Joseph Arch saw himself as a crusader and evangelist. As he himself wrote: "I was going from place to place as hard and as fast as I could, addressing meetings and forming branches of the

Union. All that stirring time I felt as if there was a living fire in me. It seemed to me that I was fulfilling a mission; that I had been raised up for the work . . . When I stood up there with all these brethren gathered together in Congress, while we sang Russell's spirit-stirring Union Hymn as with one mighty voice, I said within myself, 'Joseph Arch, you have not lived in vain, and of a surety the Lord God of Hosts is with us this day.' (51)"

In 1874 when Suffolk labourers asked for a wage increase, the farmers responded by a lock-out which spread to neighbouring counties. *The Labourers' Union Chronicle* of 21st March, 1874 recorded: "About 2,000 men are now in idleness and on the funds of the NALU—some for asking for a rise in their wages—for the sin of asking, the right to do which is absolutely denied;—some have struck because, having asked for a rise by giving a week's notice to their employers they are refused, for, as the farmers say, 'it looks like meaking us'—others, and by far the greater number, are locked out because they are members of the

The agricultural lock-out and a farmer is reduced to doing his own ploughing.

Union, and they refuse to employ them unless they withdraw . . ."

The Union spent £21,000 in strike pay, and could not survive the agricultural depression. Joseph Arch was summoned to appear before the 1882 Royal Commission on Agriculture, and he took the opportunity as a witness to express his view of unionism as a means of improving the standard of living of agricultural workers, as some of his answers indicate:

"Is your union in any way a life assurance society?— They insure for sickness, and old age, and death.

"Is it a burial club?—Yes, we allow £5 for burial.

"Is it a savings bank?—No.

"Then to what extent are its funds strike funds?— To any extent, according as the members dispose of them.

"Do you approve of strikes?—No, certainly not.

"Have you ever calculated the gain or loss resulting from a strike?—No. Strikes are sometimes a necessity, but I say they are necessary evils. I do not like them, and I think they might be avoided; and this is where the farmers would never meet us. We have tried our utmost to get a board of arbitration, and they will not meet us fairly . . . (52)."

In 1884 agricultural labourers gained the vote, and in 1885 the Norfolk labourers helped to return Joseph Arch to Parliament as their MP. MacDonald and Arch did their utmost to work with the bosses. However by 1888 trade was again improving, unemployment was falling, and some unionists were beginning to sense that the time had come to be militant. One such unionist, Tom Mann, the dockers' leader, had written in 1886: "None of the important societies [trade unions] have any policy other than that of endeavouring to keep wages from falling. The true Unionist policy of *aggression* seems entirely lost sight of; in fact the average unionist of to-day is a man with a fossilized intellect, either hopelessly apathetic, or supporting a policy that plays directly into the hands of the capitalist exploiter."

The Match Girls

In 1888 the Match Girls of Bryant and May formed a union, helped by a socialist Mrs Annie Besant. Mrs Besant compiled

Members of the Matchmakers' Union who struck for higher wages in 1888.

details of the poor wages and appalling working conditions of the Match Girls. She published the findings in an article called *White Slavery in London*. In it she called for a boycott of Bryant and May's matches. Eventually some 1,400 of the girls came out on strike. Public sympathy and some financial support was given to the girls' union. As a result the girls were given a wage increase. This was an unexpected victory for a small union of unskilled workers. It was also a warning of the great industrial strife that lay ahead. The girls' success gave strength to other organizations of the unskilled.

The "New Unionism"

Will Thorne first organized the Gasworkers and General Labourers' Union in 1887, and within two years gained the recognition of the eight-hour day even without a strike. "The

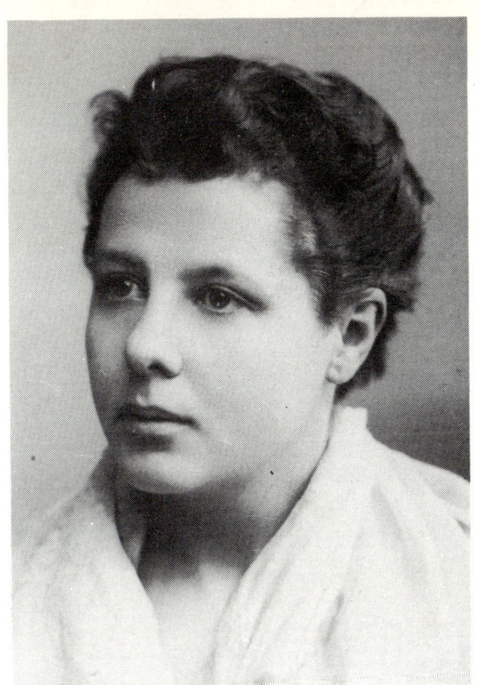

Annie Besant.

Will Thorne MP.

formation of our union was the definite establishment and the beginning of what has been termed the 'new unionism.' It was the culmination of long years of Socialist propaganda amongst the underpaid and oppressed workers. Politics had been preached to them, vague indefinite appeals to revolution, but we offered them something tangible, a definite, clearly-lighted road out of their misery, a trade union that would improve their wages and conditions; that would protect them from petty tyranny of employers . . . We showed the way to the dockers and other unskilled workers; our example and our success gave them hope. Within a short time the new unionism was in full flower. It changed the whole face of the British Trade Union Movement, a movement that had mainly consisted of reformist, liberal-minded craftsmen and skilled unionists. The growth and development of our union and the dockers and others that followed us brought to the Trade Union Congress a new force, clear-sighted and virile. It established, on a firm footing, the political Labour Movement (53)."

Dock labourers being hired at the West India Docks in London.

The Dockers' Strike

The London dockers were encouraged to strike in 1889. Casual labour at the docks brought great hardship to dockers' families. The dockers demanded a wage of 6d ($2\frac{1}{2}$p) an hour, special payment for overtime, the abolition of sub-contracting and piecework, and that a four-hour half-shift be the minimum period of employment. Their leaders were Ben Tillett, Tom Mann and John Burns. Tillett described the working conditions of his fellow-dockers thus: "To obtain employment we are driven into a shed, iron-barred from end to end, outside of which a foreman . . . walks up and down with the air of a dealer in a cattle-market, picking and choosing from a crowd of men, who, in their eagerness to obtain employment, trample each other underfoot . . . this struggling mass fought desperately and tigerishly, using the last remnants of their strength to get work for an hour or half an hour."

The *Reynolds' Newspaper* of 1st September, 1889 reported: "When the strike was first announced a fortnight ago, the number of men amounted to about 10,000. Soon the figures reached 100,000 . . . The sympathy of the stevedores was awakened. They protested and joined the dockmen. The gallant example was immediately followed by other riverside employees—shore gangs, carmen, firemen, scalers, ironworkers, coalies, 'Lumpers', biscuit-makers, and labourers of every description. As days passed the strike grew in intensity and breadth . . . Every industry was paralysed. Tens of thousands of tons of food was rotting in the ships lying in the Thames. All this was the result of union of labour interests, and though we trust that a general rising may not be necessary, it is satisfactory to have proven that labour has the destinies of the world in its own hands, and can, if it chooses, control them against all the power of capital."

The strike lasted a month, and received much publicity and support. Large sums of money were raised both in England and abroad. This enabled reasonable strike allowances to be paid. There was solidarity amongst the men and the employers were not successful in finding "blacklegs" to work. Finally Cardinal Manning, the Roman Catholic Archbishop of Westminster, helped the dockers to get what they wanted. Even *The Times* agreed that the dockers had won: "The dock labourers and their allies have won a remarkable victory. The dock companies have granted all their demands . . . the strike will remain a most significant event in the relations between capital and labour . . .

Dockers parade through the East End of London during the strike of 1889.

The hints afforded by the great strike will probably not be neglected in the future. It would not be too much to say that we may look for a large development of them in future conflicts between capital and labour. The alliance of riverside labourers, possessing various grades of skill and social standing, will probably be taken as an encouragement to carry into effect wider federations of labour (54)."

The successful strike certainly stimulated the growth of many "new unions" for unskilled workers. Wages began to rise, sometimes because of a threat rather than the actual outbreak of a strike. The leadership of the trade unions was also changing. John Burns described the delegates of the new unions at the TUC in 1890: "Physically, the 'old' unionists were much bigger than the new . . . A great number of them looked like respectable city gentlemen; wore very good coats, large watch chains, and high hats, and in many cases were of such splended build and proportions that they presented an aldermanic, not to say majestical form and dignity. Amongst the new delegates not a single one wore a tall hat. They looked workmen; they were

Ben Tillett.

John Burns.

workmen. They were not such sticklers for formality or court procedure, but were guided more by common sense."

The Taff Vale Case

Two legal decisions badly affected the trade unions in the 1900–14 period. In 1901 a strike took place on the Taff Vale Railway in South Wales. The railway company sued the Amalgamated Society of Railway Servants for damages; it was awarded £23,000. This was a disastrous blow not only for this particular union, but for the Trade Union Movement as a whole. It meant that even if a strike were successful, the cost to an individual union might be ruinous. Not until the Liberals were swept into office in 1906 in a Parliament of forty-four Labour MPs was the Taff Vale decision reversed. The Trade Union Act of that year said that the funds of unions were not liable for damages. This was an immense gain for the trade unions and put them in a privileged position.

The Osborne Case

The second blow came in 1907 when a railway worker named Osborne, a member of the Amalgamated Society of Railway Servants, objected to paying part of his membership subscription to the Labour Party. All the large unions had adopted this practice of a political levy. The Courts upheld Osborne's objection. This was a blow both to the Labour Party, which depended on union financial support, and to the unions, which needed representation in Parliament. The "Osborne Judgement" was confirmed by the House of Lords in 1909.

The TUC gave the official Trade Union view: "This decision is of a most far-reaching character . . . So long as this decision remains the law of the land, our work will be hindered and the full effects of our organization cannot be realized. The history of our parliamentary representation takes us back nearly fifty years . . . Right along . . . the trade union world had no other idea than that it was one of their objects not only to work for, but to maintain in Parliament, men representing the trade union forces of this country, and from 1874 onwards, the funds of trade unions have been applied to the purpose of paying and returning members to the House of Commons (55)." Osborne however, had made the point that there was now a new and different situation, and a new principle involved. He said: "It must be remembered that a distinct political payment is demanded, not, as previously, for one of their members to watch their trade interests in Parliament, but for the purpose of subsidizing a definite political party that includes men who have no connection with their trade, and are not necessarily even trade unionists (56)."

The 1913 Trade Union Act reversed the Osborne Judgement, however, by making a political levy by a union legal provided it was supported by a majority of the members of the union. It also allowed any individual member who objected to paying the levy, not to do so by "contracting out" when paying the union membership subscription. In practice the unions put pressure on individuals not to contract out, and the 1913 Act worked to the benefit of both the Labour Party and the Trade Union Movement.

Syndicalism

Meanwhile in the years leading up to 1914 the trade unions were becoming stronger and more militant. There was a great wave of strikes between 1910 and 1914, in which miners, railwaymen and dockers were the main groups involved. This wider militancy went under the name of syndicalism, as a result of the methods and aims proposed by Tom Mann in his monthly paper called *The Industrial Syndicalist*. In the first issue of July 1910, Mann wrote: "What is called for? What will have to be the essential conditions for the success of such a movement?

"That it should be avowedly and clearly revolutionary in aim and method.

"Revolutionary in aim, because it will be out for the abolition of the wages system, and for securing to the workers the full fruits of their labours, thereby seeking to change the system of society from Capitalist to Socialist.

"Revolutionary in method, because it will refuse to enter into any long agreements with the masters, whether with legal or State backing, or merely voluntarily; and because it will seize every chance of fighting for the general betterment . . . (57)." Tom Mann was not saying that the trade unions could do without the Labour Party, nor that they should not support it. He was claiming that the Trade Union Movement was by 1910 strong enough to achieve dominance over the capitalists even, presumably against a democratic decision to the contrary.

A demonstration of workers from the Royal Ordnance factories marches along The Embankment in London, February 1914.

"The curse of capitalism consists in this—that a handful of capitalists can compel hundreds of thousands of workers to work in such a manner and for such a wage as will please the capitalists. But this again is solely because of the inability of workers to agree upon a common form of action. The hour the workers agree and act, they become all powerful. We can settle the capitalists' strike-breaking power once and for all. We shall have no need to plead with parliamentarians to be good enough to reduce hours as the workers have been doing for a full twenty years without result. We shall be able to do this for ourselves, and there will be no power on earth to stop us (58)."

Transport workers, miners, and railwaymen had formed large, militant unions, and in 1913 Robert Smillie, the miners' leader, suggested that the three unions should act together in a "Triple Alliance". The stage was set for the Trade Union Movement to wield enormous power, but the outbreak of the First World War temporarily ended the unrest and militancy of the unions.

The Sunday school — a ray of hope for many working-class children in Victorian England.

5 Chapels and Chapel-goers

ALTHOUGH THE GENERAL IMPRESSION of the Victorian Age as a time when the churches and chapels were full and prosperous has some truth in it, it provides a false picture of the working-class attitude to organized religion. Friedrich Engels was probably near the truth when he wrote in 1844: "All the writers of the bourgeoisie are unanimous on this point, that the workers are not religious, and do not attend church (59)." Moreover, the 1851 *Religious Census* reported that the masses of the working population "are never or but seldom seen in our religious congregations."

The Primitive Methodists

However, there were some striking exceptions to this general rule. Some Nonconformist chapel congregations were substantially, and in some cases exclusively, working-class in composition. This was not true of the Congregationalists, Presbyterians, Unitarians, Quakers, or even of the Wesleyan Methodists; but it was true of some of the branches of Methodism, for example the Methodist New Connexion, the Primitive Methodists, the Bible Christians, and the Wesleyan Reformers. The Primitive Methodists were easily the largest of these four denominations, but the combined totals of attendances at the four was over half a million in 1851, and probably over a million by 1900. In addition they all had large numbers of Sunday school scholars.

Sunday Schools

In an age when many children from working-class homes were denied any formal schooling, Sunday schools made a significant contribution to providing an elementary education. Certainly Primitive Methodists saw themselves providing this role. "It was this lamentable lack of the elements of ordinary education, and the utter absence of any provision to supply the lack, that explains one of the main features of our [Primitive Methodist] early Sunday schools. While the moral and religious training of the pupils was the supreme purpose, it was nevertheless sought to inform the mind, and develop the intellect, to teach them the arts of reading, writing and arithmetic. The three R's were the rule in many schools: "It was quite customary for the school to begin in a private house; in the labourer's cottage, the miner's home, or the farmer's kitchen. A disused workshop or an old store would be utilized; a battered shed or broken down shanty at the colliery or the ironworks, the hayloft over a stable, the clubroom of a public house, the cellar of a warehouse, or the top storey of a factory (60)."

Working-class chapel-goers believed in a strict life, not only for themselves, but for their children. The following rules were to be followed in Primitive Methodist Sunday schools:

1 The children must come clean, washed and combed.
2 No child shall be admitted under four years of age, not without one of the parents or a friend duly authorized.
3 No scholar must be allowed to bring any child that requires nursing, nor any fruits or sweetmeats to eat in the school.
4 The children are not to go out during the school hours if they can avoid it; and not till after the first hour; and then they must ask permission of their teachers; and not more than one from a class must be allowed out at the same time.
5 No scholar must be allowed to take any of the school books out of the school, on any pretence whatsoever.
6 Any scholar absent three successive Sundays, cases of sickness or unavoidable necessity excepted, shall be dismissed.
7 If, after repeated reproof, any scholar be convicted of cursing, swearing, gaming, quarrelling, wilful lying, using indecent language, such shall be excluded forthwith.
8 As the chief object of this school is to promote the eternal salvation of the children, they shall, at stated times, attend divine worship in the chapel (61).

Many twentieth-century leaders of the Labour Movement like Arthur Henderson, Ellen Wilkinson and George Thomas, have often acknowleged their indebtedness to the sure foundation laid for their lives and careers by Methodist parenthood, and chapel and Sunday school influence in their youth. Working-class Methodists built up a great sense of fellowship and comradeship in their chapels. They had their revival services, open-air meetings, lovefeasts, prayer meetings and weekly class meetings. Class meetings, which were often held in each other's homes, took the following form:

Methodist Class Meeting

1 Open with singing for about three, four or five minutes.
2 Let there be three or four minutes spent in prayer.
3 Sing about two or three minutes.
4 The leader speak one or two minutes, chiefly about his own experience.
5 Let fifteen, or from that to twenty minutes be spent in conversation of the leader with the members. And to keep the attention alive, the leader, during the conversation, may if he chooses, give out one or two verses, and sing.
6 If a class has fifteen or sixteen members, the average speaking time should be about one minute with each member. If there be twenty or thirty members, the time should be less, because in speaking to one, the leader in effect, speaks to

Ellen Wilkinson.

all. In particular cases more time may be spent with any member.

7 When the speaking is concluded, sing for two or three minutes.

8 Then let the members pray in quick succession, for about one or two minutes each (62).

Methodists, men and women, were very active, and usually held more than one of the following positions in their local chapel: steward, Sunday school teacher, local preacher, class leader, secretary or treasurer to a committee or meeting. Working-class Methodists were self-taught in the arts of public speaking and administration. They had their chapel debating and mutual improvement societies, and they enjoyed their socials, concerts and outings. They often provided social and economic benefits, not only to their own chapel-goers, but to those in the area who were in need. The Whitechapel Primitive Methodist Mission in London carried this advertisement at the beginning of the twentieth century: "Social Agencies: Free Night Shelter for homeless men; Penny Dinners for necessitous adults and slum children; Poor Mans' Lawyer; Distribution of cast-off garments; Free Admission to Seaside Holiday and Convalescent Homes of needy Primitive Methodists and others at nominal charges. Home for destitute and orphan lads, also first offenders on probation; Prison and Police Court Mission; Visitation of the Poor by Sisters of the People; Day in Country Excursions; Summer Camp for Boy Crusaders and Girl Guides."

Chapel Social Work

Primitive Methodists as working-class people significantly dressed plainly. The Conference ruling ran: "In what dress shall our travelling preachers appear in public? In a plain one: the men to wear single-breasted coats, single-breasted waistcoats, and their hair in its natural form; and not to be allowed to wear pantaloons, trousers, nor white hats: and that our female preachers be patterns of plainness in all their dress. We strongly recommend it to our brethren, the stewards, local preachers, leaders and members, both male and female, in our societies to be plain in their dress (63)."

On facing page The Sunday school outing and a chance for a day out in the country for these poor children of London.

SALLY OF OUR ALLEY

A MIDSUMMER DAY

HOME SWEET HOME

TTLE ONES FROM THE COUNTRY

NOT FOR THE COUNTRY

A RAY OF LIGHT

Chapel Politics

The Nonconformists as a whole supported Gladstone and the Liberal Party, but most of the working-class chapel-goers tended to be radical in their politics, and by the 1890s many of these were determined socialists. The letter below was sent to the *Clarion*, a socialist newspaper, in 1893: "I noticed your Oldham correspondent's remarks about the *Clarion* being cheered in a Primitive Methodist Sunday school, and think he seems rather surprised about it. But if he should be in Huddersfield any Sunday . . . he would hear as hearty praise of it as he does in Oldham. We have a small band of Clarionettes in connection with our school, who are striving to show the practicability of Christianity and Socialism by proving that the foundation of both is: 'Do unto others as we would that others should do unto us'."

Toryism was regarded by working-class Methodists as a class enemy, and as such to be defeated. *The Primitive Methodist Leader* wrote on 14th December, 1905: "Labour and Liberalism are one in spirit and aim, and must act as one. Toryism is the historical and persistent foe of the labouring classes. For the sake of the million toilers of Britain we must defeat it. Every voter and non-voter is wanted in this fight. Cancel all engagements that interfere with election work. Give your nights and days to the task. Seek first, and seek only the Kingdom of God in and through this General Election."

Inevitably, by the late nineteenth century, many politically minded Methodists took their new-found talents and their zeal into secular activities and were elected to Poor Law Boards, Boards of Education, local and county councils, and a few to Parliament. Many of the early trade union leaders were Methodists, both at local and national level. Joseph Arch was an outstanding example, but the following account is perhaps indicative of the many less well-known leaders: "I was among the Primitive in the Alford Circuit for over thirty years. I worked as a local preacher for the cause of Christ . . . When the Labourers' Union first started in Alford I took a very great interest in it. As an unpaid officer I worked for a living by day, and went out at nights to lecture for the benefit of the Union . . . The year 1872 gave birth to the Labourers' Union. I, Joseph Chapman, with

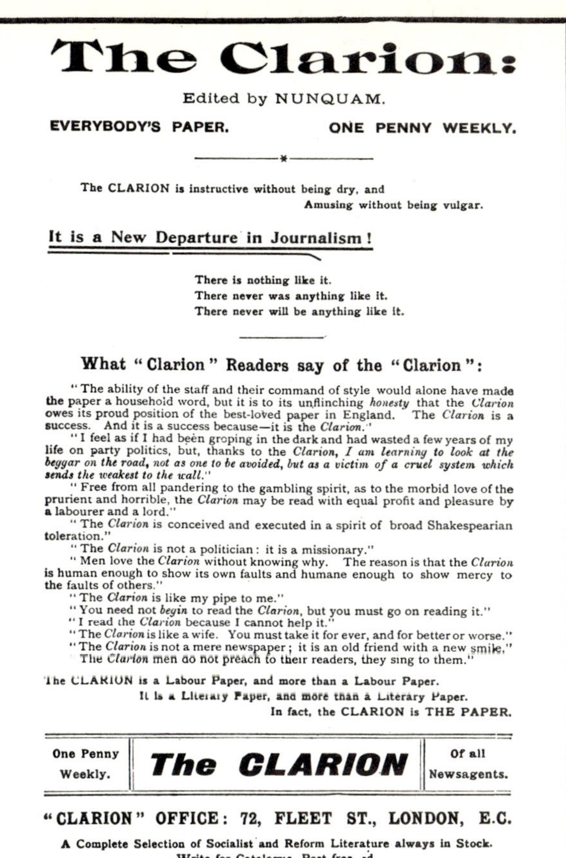

The Clarion:

Edited by NUNQUAM.

EVERYBODY'S PAPER. **ONE PENNY WEEKLY.**

The CLARION is instructive without being dry, and
Amusing without being vulgar.

It is a New Departure in Journalism!

There is nothing like it.
There never was anything like it.
There never will be anything like it.

What "Clarion" Readers say of the "Clarion":

"The ability of the staff and their command of style would alone have made the paper a household word, but it is to its unflinching *honesty* that the *Clarion* owes its proud position of the best-loved paper in England. The *Clarion* is a success. And it is a success because—it is the *Clarion.*"

"I feel as if I had been groping in the dark and had wasted a few years of my life on party politics, but, thanks to the *Clarion, I am learning to look at the beggar on the road, not as one to be avoided, but as a victim of a cruel system which sends the weakest to the wall.*"

"Free from all pandering to the gambling spirit, as to the morbid love of the prurient and horrible, the *Clarion* may be read with equal profit and pleasure by a labourer and a lord."

"The *Clarion* is conceived and executed in a spirit of broad Shakespearian toleration."

"The *Clarion* is not a politician: it is a missionary."

"Men love the *Clarion* without knowing why. The reason is that the *Clarion* is human enough to show its own faults and humane enough to show mercy to the faults of others."

"The *Clarion* is like my pipe to me."

"You need not *begin* to read the *Clarion*, but you must go on reading it."

"I read the *Clarion* because I cannot help it."

"The *Clarion* is like a wife. You must take it for ever, and for better or worse."

"The *Clarion* is not a mere newspaper; it is an old friend with a new smile."

"The *Clarion* men do not preach to their readers, they sing to them."

The CLARION is a Labour Paper, and more than a Labour Paper.
It is a Literary Paper, and more than a Literary Paper.
In fact, the CLARION is THE PAPER.

One Penny Weekly.	**The CLARION**	Of all Newsagents.

"CLARION" OFFICE: 72, FLEET ST., LONDON, E.C.

A Complete Selection of Socialist and Reform Literature always in Stock.
Write for Catalogue, Post free, 1d.

The front page of the *Clarion*. In its hey-day, the *Clarion* reached a circulation of 100,000.

Joseph Arch and William Banks of Boston, gave our tongues, our heads, our hearts, our influence in the maturing of the above Union."

Practically all the leaders of the Northumberland and Durham, and the Nottingham and Derbyshire miners in the nineteenth century were active Methodists. Methodist structure, practices, and personnel obviously played an influential part in the rise of the Labour Movement. We have noted how the Methodist practices of having class meetings and the 1d a week class money were copied and used by the Reform Clubs in the 1790s, and by the National Union of the Working Classes in 1830, and by the Chartists in the 1840s. The Chartists also adopted the Primitive Methodist custom of holding large

William Booth (right) with his son, Bramwell.

open-air gatherings in a field, called camp-meetings. Several leading Chartists, co-operators and trade unionists were Methodists. The tradition of singing a hymn has survived in many trade union and Labour Party gatherings until quite recently, largely because of the Labour Movement's indebtedness to the early leadership provided by Methodists.

The Salvation Army

Primitive Methodism could certainly have claimed to be a working-class movement in its own right. The Salvation Army, however, whilst meeting both religious and social needs amongst the labouring classes, did not see itself as a part of the Labour Movement. But the Salvation Army certainly made many converts amongst the working class. William Booth, the founder of The Army, himself wrote that his early assistants were all "genuine working men. One has been a blacksmith, another a navvy, another a policeman, another a sailor, and the remainder have been engaged in similar callings. Consequently, they can speak to the working man as belonging to the same class, illustrating their exhortations with their own experience (64)."

The Labour Church

There was even a Labour Church. It was only a small movement begun in 1891 by John Trevor, who declared: "God is in the Labour Movement. This is the word of our prophecy . . . The great religious movement of our time is the movement for the emancipation of labour . . . The Labour Church is based on the following principles:

1 That the Labour Movement is a religious movement.
2 That the religion of the Labour Movement is not a class religion, but unites members of all classes in working for the abolition of commercial slavery.
3 That the religion of the Labour Movement is not sectarian or dogmatic, but free religion leaving each man free to develop his own relations with the Power that brought him into being.
4 That the emancipation of Labour can only be realized so far as men learn both the economic and moral laws of God, and heartily endeavour to obey them.
5 That the development of personal character and the improvement of social conditions are both essential to man's emancipation from moral and social bondage (65)."

A Labour Church Union was established in 1893 with some twenty-five chapels nearly all in Yorkshire and Lancashire. The Labour Church had its own hymn book and Sunday schools, but its services were unconventional with few prayers or Bible readings, and political addresses rather than sermons.

Ben Tillett, the dockers' leader, was a popular speaker at Labour Churches. The following extract describes the opening of Barrow's Labour Church in 1892: "We opened our church on December 18th as announced. Ben Tillett was advertized to conduct the services; but owing to the outbreak of a strike among the dockers at Bristol, he was unable to be present. I am afraid the cause of Labour in Barrow would have received its death-blow, had it not been for Comrade Robson, who undertook to go on with the services which were held in the Town Hall at 3 p.m. and 7 p.m. . . . We had made up our mind it was going to be a miserable failure on account of Ben Tillett's absence; but thanks to Comrade Robson and to the band and choir we have launched the Labour Church in Barrow most successfully (66)."

However, the Labour Churches did not survive the First World War. Indeed many of them declined after the formation of the Labour Party in 1906, for one of the underlying motivations of the Labour Churches was to provide a religious unity to the socialist organizations which preceded the Labour Party.

The reform meeting in Hyde Park.

6 *Labour and Labourers*

The Manhood Suffrage and Vote by Ballot Association

AS WE HAVE SEEN, the remnants of the Chartist Movement struggled on into the 1850s. In 1862 a national working-class organization was set up. It was known as the Manhood Suffrage and Vote by Ballot Association emphasizing two of the Chartist demands. The Association appealed to all trade unionists and working men to support it: "Our object is, therefore, to create an organization for the purpose of obtaining our rights as citizens; or, in other words, our just share of political power. These objects sought to be obtained by the present organization are precise and definite—namely, registered manhood suffrage by the ballot. Upon these two great principles we take our stand, and invite the whole of the Trade Unionists of this country to co-operate with us until our agitation is crowned with success . . . (67)."

The National Reform League

In 1865 the Association largely merged into the National Reform League, which included some middle-class supporters. However, it was still a predominantly working-class movement seeking to gain a political voice for the labourer. The leader of the League was a barrister called Edmund Beales. He and his supporters tried to hold a mass meeting in Hyde Park, London, in July 1866. The authorities forbad the meeting and a large police force was on duty to prevent any entry to the park. The leaders turned back, but a large portion of the crowd ". . . smashed down the railings of the park in sight of the police, and entered the ground cheering and waving . . . and in a few minutes several thousands had entered the park. Encounters between the police and mob now became rife, the former using their truncheons freely, and the latter stones and other missiles (67)."

The Home Secretary of the Conservative Government, Mr Spencer Walpole, made a deal with Beales that the Reform League could use Hyde Park for its meetings if the League would ensure good conduct. As a result the League felt that it had gained enormously in strength and prestige. Early in 1867 members of the League lobbied MPs at the House of Commons for the extension of the franchise, and the General Council of the League passed this threatening resolution. "Unless a satisfactory prospect is held out in Parliament of the working classes being universally enfranchised upon the principles of the Reform League, it will be necessary to consider the propriety of these classes adopting a universal cessation from labour until their political rights are conceded (69)."

The League, which had approximately 600 branches, with 100 in London, arranged another mass meeting to be held in Hyde Park in May 1867. Mr Spencer Walpole and the Government unwisely decided to forbid the meeting and enlisted the aid of thousands of special constables to enforce its will. The League however, resolved to go ahead with plans to hold the meeting, and on the day a vast crowd, estimated at over 100,000, moved into the park, and it was not resisted. Some ten platforms of speakers were erected. The police were hissed at but no violence took place. As the *Reynolds' Newspaper*, a newspaper for the working class, put it: "the triumph of the working men was complete and bloodless." For a second time the Government had been humiliated and the League's prestige enhanced. The episode of 7th May at Hyde Park was a reversal of the Kennington Common event of the Chartists in 1848. Of course the Government could have got its way by using armed force, but doubtless it realized that such action would probably have led to bloodshed and possibly even revolution. However, having given in to the meeting the Government could not easily resist the League's demand to widen the franchise. The League's activities were probably one of the factors which led to the passing of the second Parliamentary Reform Act in August 1867, which nearly doubled the size of the electorate. This act gave the working-class man a vote in the town, but not in the country constituency.

The London Working Men's Association

Another working-class organization which could claim to have assisted in swelling the crowds at Hyde Park was the London Working Men's Association (the LWMA). In 1867 the organization issued a manifesto calling for a national movement to bring about the election of working-class men to Parliament.

"The working men selected as candidates for the representation of industrial interests should . . . be men who have been hard workers in the cause of industrial progress—not mere word-spinners—who have for years past made sacrifices, personal and pecuniary, for the cause they advocated . . . They should be men whose general abilities, character, and demeanour should be such that no one of their colleagues, however aristocratic, should be ashamed to associate with them in Westminster Hall. There are hundreds of such working men to be found (70)."

The LWMA called upon co-operative societies, trade unions and other working-class organizations to sponsor suitable candidates, and partly as a result of these efforts a number of working-class candidates stood in the 1868 general election. These included W Cremer of the Carpenters at Warwick, E Greening, the co-operator at Halifax, and George Howell, secretary of the National Reform League at Aylesbury. However, none of these was successful. Neither the National Reform League nor the LWMA survived for long. Their place was taken by a new body, the Labour Representation League, founded in 1869 largely by the trade unions. It sought to promote the candidature of working-class men not only to Parliament, but to local councils and other representative bodies. In 1871 the Labour Representation League, whose secretary was George Howell, issued this address: "Fellow working men, we ask you to consider the following facts— There are about twenty millions of persons in the United Kingdom belonging to the working classes . . .

The Labour Representation League

"There are also in Great Britain ten millions or thereabouts of all other classes, viz: nobility, landed gentry, the various professions, employers of labour and others.

"In the House of Commons there are 658 members, whose business it is to make the laws under which the whole of the people of all classes live. These 658 men are supposed to understand the circumstances of the various classes, and to shape their laws, so as to impartially promote the interests of all. Strange to say, however, every one of the 658 belongs to the middle and upper classes—Labour had not one direct representative—there is not in the House of Commons ONE MAN whose life has been

George Howell.

Thomas Burt.

spent in the workshop in intimate daily experience of the working man's trials, or who has been engaged in those struggles in connection with labour, upon which he founds his hopes of future regeneration.

"Working men; do not forget you can alter all this if you will . . . We call on you as a paramount and pressing duty, to return qualified men of your own order to Parliament (71)."

In 1872 Gladstone's reforming Liberal Government passed the Ballot Act making voting secret, and in 1874 there was a general election. In this election the Labour Representation League supported thirteen working-class candidates, two of whom, perhaps surprisingly, were elected; Alexander MacDonald, the miners' leader, was elected for Stafford and Thomas Burt, another miners' representative for Morpeth in Northumberland. One of Burt's Campaign songs went:

> So they want Tommy Burt to be thor MP—
> A man thit they knaa, an' a man thit for sure
> Winnet easily forget to luik efter the poor.

These two men were the first "Labour" MPs. At long last the labouring classes could feel that they had at least a voice of their own in Parliament. It was a beginning on the long road leading to political power. Eleven of the League's thirteen "Labour" candidates were trade unionists, and by 1874 the Labour Representation League had become virtually a trade union body. As such it was particularly interested in the repeal of the Criminal Law Amendment Act which did not allow picketing in strikes.

On facing page Karl Marx, the founder of international Communism.

When in 1875 Disraeli's Conservative Government abolished the Criminal Law Amendment Act, much of the fire and spirit went out of the League, and it began to lose support. Clearly the trade union interest was more a dominant feature than any desire to build a broadly based working-class party. Moreover, lack of finance made the League's task difficult; a candidate had to pay all his own election expenses, returning officers' fees, a deposit, and if elected, his own maintenance as an MP. The trade unions were not yet wealthy enough to contribute. Until 1880, the majority of the labouring classes still looked to Gladstone and the Liberal Party to champion their interests, prompting Freidrich Engels to write that the working class had become "the tail of the great Liberal Party". However working-class disillusionment grew with Gladstone's Government's reluctance to embark on a further programme of social and political reform, and the apparent continuation of Disraeli's imperialistic policies in Egypt and South Africa.

Marx and Marxism

At this stage perhaps we ought to pause to refer to Engels' life-long German friend, Karl Marx (1818–83). The two of them wrote *The Communist Manifesto* in 1848, and in the following year Marx settled in London where he spent the rest of his life, mostly in poverty. He wrote a large number of works; his most famous being *Capital*. Volume one of this great work was published in 1867, and the whole three volumes were translated into English in 1884. Marx had little contact with the British Labour Movement, except through the International Working Men's Association. His writings, however, undoubtedly had great influence. Here are a few of his memorable sentences:

"The history of all hitherto existing society is the history of class struggles . . . Society as a whole is more and more splitting up into great hostile camps, into two great classes directly facing each other; Bourgeoisie and Proletariat . . . We have seen that the first step in the revolution by the working class is to raise the proletariat to the position of ruling class, to win the battle for democracy. The proletariat will use its political supremacy to wrest, by degrees, all capital from the bourgeoisie, to centralize all instruments of production in the hands of the State, i.e. of the proletariat as the ruling class; and to increase the total of productive forces as rapidly as possible (72)."

The Social Democratic Federation

The Democratic Federation was founded in 1881 by Henry M Hyndman, a wealthy stockbroker, who published *England for All* in the same year; his ideas owed much to Marx's teachings. To begin with, the Federation had a radical rather than a socialist basis. In 1884 it took the name of the Social Democratic Federation (SDF), and as such was the first socialist political body to exist in Britain, and the first socialist organization of any size since the disappearance of Owenism. Its programme given here was certainly ambitious and far reaching, and owed a lot to the teachings of Karl Marx.

"Object: The establishment of a free condition of society based on the principle of POLITICAL EQUALITY with EQUAL SOCIAL RIGHTS for all and the complete EMANCIPATION OF LABOUR.

Programme:

1 ALL OFFICERS or ADMINISTRATORS to be elected by EQUAL DIRECT ADULT SUFFRAGE, and to be paid by the community.
2 LEGISLATION BY THE PEOPLE, in such wise that no project of law shall become legally binding till accepted by the Majority of the People.
3 The ABOLITION of a STANDING ARMY and the ESTABLISHMENT of a NATIONAL CITIZEN FORCE; the PEOPLE to decide on PEACE OR WAR.
4 All Education, higher no less than elementary, to be FREE, COMPULSORY, SECULAR and INDUSTRIAL for all alike.

Hyndman addressing the unions in Trafalgar Square.

5 The ADMINISTRATION of JUSTICE to be FREE and GRATUITOUS for all Members of Society.
6 The LAND, with all the MINES, RAILWAYS, and other MEANS OF TRANSIT to be declared and treated as COLLECTIVE or COMMON PROPERTY.
7 IRELAND and all other parts of the Empire to have LEGISLATIVE INDEPENDENCE.
8 The PRODUCTION OF WEALTH to be regulated by SOCIETY in the common interest of all its Members.
9 The MEANS OF PRODUCTION, DISTRIBUTION and EXCHANGE to be declared and treated as COLLECTIVE or COMMON PROPERTY (73)."

The SDF attracted some trade unionists, but many of them were offended by Hyndman's upper-middle-class image; he belonged to a wealthy family, had been educated at Eton and Cambridge, and dressed in a flamboyant manner. He was opposed in particular by Tom Mann, who was later to make his mark as a trade union and labour leader. Mann recalled his early days in the SDF thus: "I threw myself into the movement with all the energy at my command . . . I found my bearings very quickly on fraternizing with, and listening to the speeches of John Burns, H M Hyndman . . . and many others with whom I came into contact . . . John Burns and I became close friends and good comrades . . . He had a splendid voice and a very effective and business-like way of putting a case . . . Surprisingly fluent, with a voice that could fill the largest hall or theatre, and, if the wind were favourable, could reach a twenty-thousand audience in the parks, etc, he was undoubtedly the most remarkable propagandist speaker in the country.

H M Hyndman

"Hyndman was a very different personality in the early days of propaganda—for he took his turn regularly at outdoor gatherings as well as indoor—his essential bourgeois appearance attracted much attention. His tall hat, the frock coat, and the long beard drew the curious-minded who would not have spent time listening to one in workman's attire. At almost every meeting he addressed, Hyndman would cynically thank the audience for 'so generously supporting my class'. Indeed, he brought in 'my class' to an objectionable degree. It seemed to some of us that it would have been better if he could have dropped this reference, but none of us doubted his whole-souled advocacy of Socialism as he conceived it . . . I am convinced, however, that Hyndman's bourgeois mentality made it impossible for him to estimate the worth of industrial organization correctly. For many years he attached no importance whatever to the trade-union movement, and his influence told disastrously on others (74)."

William Morris and The Socialist League

Another body of opponents of Hyndman was led by William Morris, the gifted and successful artist, poet, designer and writer, whose hatred of the ugliness and waste of the Industrial Revolution led him to become a socialist and a member of the SDF. But Morris and his friends so resented Hyndman's autocratic leadership of the SDF that in December 1884, they withdrew their membership and formed a rival organization which they called the Socialist League. This body had for a time considerable educational influence, particularly through the writings of William Morris, who had an impressive way of put-

On facing page William Morris — founder of the Socialist League.

ting his ideas: "I am asked if I believe in Marx's theory of value. To speak quite frankly, I do not know what Marx's theory of value is, and I'm damned if I want to know. Truth to say, my friends, I have tried to understand Marx's theory, but political economy is not in my line, and much of it appears to me to be dreary rubbish. But I am, I hope, a Socialist none the less. It is enough political economy for me to know that the idle class is rich and the working class is poor, and that the rich are rich because they rob the poor. That I know because I see it with my own eyes. I need no book to convince me of it (75)."

When William Morris resigned from the Socialist League in 1889 the movement declined rapidly. As the result of internal differences, it became another casualty along the road to a united and strong labour party. The SDF, however, survived the split, and succeeded in electing several councillors to local government. However, its candidates at parliamentary elections did not poll well, in fact, the SDF never succeeded in electing a Member of Parliament. The movement made itself look ridiculous and became unpopular by accepting financial help for its candidates from the Conservative Party ("Tory gold") in order to reduce the Liberal vote in some constituencies. The paid membership of the SDF probably never exceeded a thousand, and these were middle class, or at least the working-class elite, readers and thinkers, rather than typical labourers. However,

the movement supported the cause of the unemployed and the poorly paid, and organized processions and meetings. In particular it provided much of the leadership for the successful Dockers' Strike of 1889. Although the SDF did not harvest any fruits of this victory itself, the Labour Movement as a whole did. Ben Tillett, one of the dockers' leaders, wrote that the strike "marked the beginning of that close alliance in thought and purpose between the trade union movement and the socialist movement which produced, in due course, the Labour Party."

The SDF and the Dockers' Strike

In 1884 the third Parliamentary Reform Act was passed. At last the franchise was extended to include all male householders in the countryside, thus putting the agricultural labourer on level terms with the artisan. In the general election of 1885, eleven working-class candidates were returned to the House of Commons. But they had a Lib-Lab label, and actually sat with the Liberals in the House.

In 1887 the Ayrshire miners carried this resolution: "The time has come for the formation of a Labour Party in the House of Commons, and we hereby agree to assist in returning one or more members to represent the miners of Scotland at the first available opportunity (76)."

James Keir Hardie

In 1888 James Keir Hardie stood as Labour candidate in Mid-Lanark, and said, "I ask you to return to Parliament a man of yourselves, who being poor, can feel for the poor, and whose whole interest lies in the direction of securing for you a better and a happier lot . . . (77)." Hardie had himself worked in the mines since he was ten years old, and had been brought up in conditions of extreme poverty. He went to night school, became a part-time journalist, and a spokesman for the miners. He was a strict and avowed Nonconformist, a teetotaller, a pacifist and a socialist. His whole philosophy of life was uncompromising, but totally committed to what he believed to be right. In the 1888 election he only polled 617 votes, but in the same year the Scottish Labour Party was formed, with Hardie as secretary. Hardie and the Scottish Labour Party concentrated their propaganda largely upon the need for a minimum wage, the legal limitation of hours of work, and "the right to work." Other local Labour Parties were formed in Lancashire, Yorkshire and the

The Scottish Labour Party

Keir Hardie, the miner who became one of the first Labour MPs.

North East. Clearly a new movement for labour representation was beginning to form outside and apart from the SDF.

In the election of 1892, Keir Hardie was elected for West Ham. That such an outspoken socialist and labourer should be a Member of Parliament was seen as an outrage to decency by many people as the following contemporary newspaper extracts reveal: "[Mr Keir Hardie] drove up to the House in defiance of all its ancient traditions in a toil-stained working suit with a cloth cap on his head and accompanied by a noisy brass band . . . followed by a noisy and disreputable throng from the dockside slums, which included many undesirable foreign elements . . ." "Precincts sacred to the topper violated by the new Member for West Ham . . ." "The working class comes to Parliament in trousers fringed at the heel . . ." "A spectacle never before witnessed in the thoroughfares leading to Westminster, bringing the great traditions of the Mother of Parliaments, at a time when the streets were lined by thousands awaiting the arrival of the Queen, into such disrepute that the members of the Opposition are considering whether it did not constitute a breach of privilege . . . (78)."

Two other independent, though less flamboyant, "Labour" candidates were also successful at this election, John Burns, an ex-member of the SDF for Battersea, and J Havelock Wilson for Middlesbrough. In addition there were some twelve Lib-Lab MPs, including George Howell of the old Labour Representation League, and Joseph Arch, the leader of the Agricultural Labourers Union.

The Bradford Conference 1893

There were many people who wanted to increase the representation of "Labour" in the House of Commons. So a conference was arranged to meet at Bradford in January 1893, to be attended by delegates from labour and socialist clubs and parties with a view to forming a national Labour party. One hundred and twenty representatives assembled. "Mr Keir Hardie, MP and Mr Ben Tillett [Alderman of the London County Council] were the most prominent speakers—the former being elected president. At the outset of the proceedings the name to be adopted was the subject of keen discussion, and it was only after a long debate that the title of the 'Socialist Labour Party' was abandoned; and the object of the party was declared to be 'to secure the collective ownership of all the means of production, distribution and exchange.' The programme ultimately agreed to . . . include the following points; the abolition of overtime, piecework, and child labour, an eight hours working day, adult suffrage, second ballots, the payment of members, and of election expenses, the abolition of the monarchy, and of the House of Lords, shorter Parliaments, the abolition of indirect taxation and a graduated income tax (79)."

The Independent Labour Party

The name adopted by the conference for the new party was the Independent Labour Party (ILP). The SDF had sent delegates to the conference, but refused to merge with the ILP because it said the programme was not sufficiently revolutionary! The cause of socialism was defended at Westminster by Keir Hardie, virtually single-handed. In February 1893, he opposed the Queen's Speech, demanding that the Government pay attention to the conditions of the unemployed: "We are now discussing an Address of Thanks to Her Majesty for her Speech. I want to ask the Government what have the unemployed to thank Her Majesty for in the Speech which has been submitted to the House? Their case is overlooked and ignored; they are left out as if they did not exist. Their misery and their sufferings could not be greater, but there is no mention of them in the Queen's Speech (80)."

The Clarion Movement

Hardie edited *The Labour Leader*, a weekly journal which was an effective medium of socialist propaganda, and the *Clarion* newspaper also gave strong support to the ILP. Clarion vans toured the country and Clarion cycling clubs, Clarion dramatic societies, and even Clarion scouts were founded and drew many people into the influence of socialism. The early days of the ILP had a strong emotional and crusading appeal. Many of its supporters were chapel-goers, and their religious missioning fervour was reflected in their political activities. It was common for the song "The Red Flag" to be sung at ILP meetings:

> With heads uncovered swear we all
> To bear it onward till we fall;
> Come dungeon dark or gallows grim
> This song shall be our parting hymn.
>
> Then raise the scarlet standard high,
> Within its shade we'll live and die;
> Though cowards flinch, and traitors sneer,
> We'll keep the Red Flag flying here.

In the 1895 general election however, the ILP suffered a severe setback. Hardie lost his seat, and no other ILP candidate of the twenty-nine that stood won. Burns and Wilson who had not joined the ILP, retained their seats. Hardie and the ILP were eventually rescued by the South Wales miners who went on strike in 1898 for six months, and looked to the ILP to champion their cause. They adopted Hardie as candidate for Merthyr, where he was elected in 1900, a seat which he held for the rest of his life. The ILP had some success in local government elections, and by 1900 had over one hundred councillors, sixty representatives on school boards, and fifty on the Poor Law boards of guardians.

The great weakness of the ILP was that it had no official connection with the trade unions, and the latter had now become by far the most powerful and wealthy of the Labour

George Bernard Shaw, playwright and member of the Fabian Society, as caricatured by Sir Bernard Partridge.

organizations. In the view of George Bernard Shaw, the unions were still the most effective means of getting working-class men elected to Parliament. "The establishment of a great number of unions in formerly unorganized trades has trebled the numbers, increased the political power and responsibility of the Trade Union organization . . . Attempts have been made by Socialists to establish societies to relieve the unions of their political duty; at a General Election the union could put up 2,000 voters for every single voter of the most successful of their rivals . . . The money difficulty does not exist for unions. A penny a week from every member of a trade union would produce £300,000. This shows how easily the larger unions alone could provide £30,000 to finance 50 Labour candidates at £600 apiece . . . Representation of the working classes at the General Election will depend on the trade unions, not on the Socialist bodies. The Fabian Society, the Social Democratic Federation, and the Independent Labour Party have not the slightest prospect of mustering enough money. Their part will be to provide the agitation which will enable the trade union leaders to obtain the support of the rank and file (81)."

The Influence of the TUC

For many years the majority of trade unionists had not seen the need for independent labour representation in Parliament, let alone for socialist MPs. But the action of the South Wales miners in adopting Hardie was evidence of a change of mind. In 1899 the TUC resolved to hold a special conference of all

On facing page Sidney and Beatrice Webb, leading members of the Fabian Society, pictured here in later life.

working-class organizations to secure more labour representation in Parliament. Trade unionists were beginning to appreciate the advantage of parliamentary representation not to further socialism, but simply to protect the trade union interest. The conference assembled in London, in February 1900, with delegates from the ILP, the SDF, the trade unions, the Co-operative Movement, and from the Fabians.

The Fabians

The Fabian Society had been founded in 1884. (It got its name from the Roman general Fabius, who believed in patient preparation and the avoidance of pitched battles.) The Society had some famous members, such as George Bernard Shaw, Annie Besant, Sidney and Beatrice Webb. They were all middle-class, intellectual socialists, who were convinced that a capitalist society was not only unjust but inefficient. They believed that capitalism was gradually being destroyed and that by gradual progress, socialism was inevitable. The primary aim of the Society was to convince men of the truth of the socialist case, and as such it was a fact-finding and fact-dispersing body, which organized lectures and research and publications. Beatrice Webb wrote: "the Fabians' aim was to make thinking persons socialistic rather than to organize unthinking persons into socialist societies." Fabians often took an active part in local affairs and several were elected to local councils.

The Fabians sent representatives to the London Conference. The SDF wanted the formation of a socialist party in the House of Commons, but Keir Hardie and the ILP wanted to increase the number of working-class Members who would show their ". . . readiness to co-operate with any party which for the time being may be engaged in promoting legislation in the direct interest of labour, and be equally ready to associate themselves with any party in opposing measures having an opposite tendency (82)."

The Labour Representation Committee

This resolution was carried. The Conference proceeded to form a Labour Representation Committee consisting of two ILP members, two SDF members, one Fabian and seven trade unionists. At long last socialists and trade unionists were united in the political field, and the following optimistic report of the inauguration of the Labour Representation Committee (LRC) appeared in the *Clarion*: "At last there is a United Labour Party, or perhaps it would be safer to say, a little cloud, no bigger than a man's hand, which may grow into a United Labour Party . . . The Conference has . . . demonstrated that half-a-million workers see the necessity for direct representation in Parliament [and] half-a-million workers are determined that when they have sent representatives to Parliament, those representatives should work harmoniously together to further the interests of Labour. Some optimistic views as to the result of the Conference have been expressed . . . The weak point about the United Labour Party is that no organized attempt is to be made to collect funds for election expenses and for the payment of their members . . . Of course, it is impossible yet to say what the intentions of the new party are. There is no programme formulated. But it is hoped that they will steer clear of entanglements with the official Liberal Party . . . (83)."

In fact the Labour Representation Committee itself was neither a trade union nor a socialist party, and individual trade unions were slow to join it at first. However, the Taff Vale Judgement of 1901 awakened political interest amongst unionists. Ramsay MacDonald, secretary of the LRC, wrote to the trade unions: "the recent decisions in the House of Lords should convince the unions that a labour party in Parliament is an

Ramsay MacDonald — a leading member of the ILP, he became the first Labour Prime Minister in 1924.

immediate necessity." The unions were beginning to recognize this and contributed to a LRC fund for the payment of MPs. But progress was slow. In the general election of 1900, two LRC candidates were elected, another won a by-election at Clitheroe in 1902, and another, Arthur Henderson, was elected in 1903. The LRC began to hold annual conferences and to appear each year more like a party, and at the 1905 Conference a definite socialist commitment was carried: ". . . the Labour Representation Committee hereby declares that its ultimate object shall be the obtaining for the workers the full results of their labour by the overthrow of the present competitive system of capitalism and the institution of a system of public ownership of all the means of production, distribution and exchange (84)."

The real breakthrough came with the 1906 general election (and the great Liberal landslide) when twenty-nine LRC candidates, and one who joined forces after the election, were elected to the House of Commons. These successes were largely due to an electoral Lib-Lab agreement. As a result of this, the LRC was given a free hand in some thirty constituencies, and in return the LRC agreed to support some Liberal candidates, and to support a future Liberal government. As John Burns said of the twenty-nine successful LRC candidates: "many of them were elected by Radical enthusiasm, Liberal votes and Trade Union funds." However, as MPs they had much in common; they were all of working-class origin, many had had long careers as trade union officials, and nearly all were Nonconformists. In addition to the LRC MPs, the miners' groups had elected fourteen "Labour" Members, and there were a further dozen Lib-Labs.

The Labour Party

The Labour Representation Committee's MPs in the House were a party, and they elected Keir Hardie as chairman, Ramsay MacDonald as secretary, and Arthur Henderson as chief whip, and significantly took the name of the Labour Party. The new party found that it could support much of the Liberal Government's programme, for example the Provision of School Meals Act of 1908, Old Age Pensions 1908, and National Insurance 1911. Some socialists in the country were unhappy at this apparent Lib-Lab alliance and in 1911 a new British Socialist Party (forerunner of the British Communist Party) was formed, but it never prospered; whereas the Labour Party had come to stay. The Labour Party not only survived the financial burden of two general elections in one year (1910), but, since joining forces with the miners' Members from 1909, increased its total numerical strength in the House to forty in January 1910 and forty-two in December 1910.

The twenty-nine LRC candidates elected to the House of Commons in 1906.

The introduction of payment to MPs in 1911 (£400 per annum) eased matters for the Labour Party, as did the Trade Union Act of 1913. This act made the systematic payment of a political levy by the unions to the Labour Party legal, and thereby ensured a constant and plentiful supply of funds. From 1911 the Labour Party had its own newspaper, the *Daily Herald*, which flourished under the editorship of George Lansbury, a future leader of the Party.

In these early years of the Labour Party the strongest electoral support came from areas of mining and heavy industry like South Wales, Durham and Clydeside, and also from areas of great poverty, such as parts of the East End of London. After the First World War the electoral appeal of the Labour Party was to widen, and gradually as the Liberal Party declined, the Labour Party was to grow to supplant it as the alternative government to Conservative.

As we have seen, the birth of the Labour Party had been made possible by the final coming together of intellectual socialists and trade unionists. This association inevitably brought strains and stresses, but it was a "marriage" that was to survive and thrive. The formation of the Labour Party was a major achievement of the working-class movement, but the labouring classes needed, and acknowledged their need of, some middle-class support and commitment.

Part of the front page from the first *Daily Herald*, January 25th, 1911.

The Daily Herald.

No. 1. LONDON, WEDNESDAY, JANUARY 25, 1911. PRICE ONE HALFPENNY.

To "ONE AND ALL."

What is this—the sound and rumour?
What is this that all men hear,
Like the wind in hollow valleys
When the storm is drawing near;
Like the rolling on of ocean
In the eventide of fear?—
'Tis the People marching on.

* * * *

Men of the L.S.C.

What nobler inspirer for the hour and the object—your modest, legitimate demand for a shorter working day—than the author of the above, that noble Old English Master Printer, William Morris, who treated

is a Labour Party in the House, and it holds supreme power.

On we march, then—we, the workers,
And the rumour that ye hear
Is the blended soul of battle
And deliverance drawing near,
For the hope of every creature
Is the banner that we bear:

50—48.

Yours, fellow workers, in the hope that conquers. W. F. REAN.

STRIKING PARAGRAPHS.

WE have arrived. At last we have a daily paper of our own. If we differ at all from the

We are surprised to see, in one of the letters issued by the Master Printers' Association, that employers who concede the men's terms may be made to suffer for their temerity. Is this a threat?

—:o:—

One of the most conspicuous features of the dispute has been the loyalty of the L.S.C. members. The notices have been tendered almost without exception. In only one instance has it come to our knowledge that certain members of the chapel failed to respond to the call. The proprietors of that establishment have decided that they will convert the establishment into an "open house." Here let it be known, once and for all, that the question of the "open house" will be fought as strenuously as the hours question itself.

7 *Epilogue*

BY 1911 the population of England and Wales was 36,000,000—four times the 1801 figure. Medical advances such as the discovery and use of anaesthetics and antiseptics, public health legislation and better and more varied supplies of food had all helped to cut the death rate from 22.3 per 1,000 in 1871 to 13.8 in 1911. Such things as ready-made clothes, cheaper bread, and higher wages contributed to make domestic life easier and happier for many. The Factory and Workshop Consolidation Act of 1901 brought together all that was best in previous nineteenth-century legislation. The 1902 Education Act led each local education authority to provide elementary and secondary education for all.

Apart from parliamentary legislation, movements supported by all classes such as the Public Health movement, and philanthropic work generally, must take a great deal of the credit for the general improvement in the lot of the masses. However, distinctively "self-help" working-class movements which collectively made up the Labour Movement had also played a major role.

After 1850 the Labour Movement had moderated its approach somewhat, so that instead of rebelling it had tried to organize its forces within the capitalist and industrialist society, and earn the respect of capitalists because of its own respectability. We have seen that in the second half of the nineteenth century the leadership of the Labour Movement had passed to the skilled workers, and an alliance of Liberalism and Labour was a significant compromise in earning this respect and respectability. Parliament's gradual concessions in extending the franchise had encouraged the Labour Movement to adopt peaceful rather than violent methods.

Despite all the progress and all the achievements, however, a great deal of poverty still existed at the beginning of the twentieth century. Charles Booth's survey *Life and Labour of the People of London*, published between 1889 and 1907, revealed terrible social conditions in the metropolis: "Houses of three rooms, houses of two rooms, houses of one room—houses set back against a wall or back to back, fronting it may be on a narrow footway, with posts at each end and a gutter down the middle. Small courts contrived to utilize some space in the rear and approached by an archway under the building which fronts the street." Shortly after Charles Booth's first revelations his namesake (but no relation), William Booth, General of the Salvation Army, published a book *In Darkest England and the Way Out.* In this work he calculated that there were about three millions of men, women and children, the "submerged tenth" he called them, who lived below the standard of the London cab horse which "when he's down he is helped up, and while he lives he has food, shelter and work. That, although a humble standard is at present absolutely unattainable by millions, literally by millions of our fellow-men and women."

Seebohm Rowntree undertook a survey of the city of York in 1901 entitled *Poverty: A Study of Town Life*. This revealed that 28 per cent of the people of York lived below the minimum poverty line; and those families which lived on the poverty line, "must never spend a penny on a railway fare or omnibus. They must never purchase a half-penny newspaper, or spend a penny to buy a ticket for a popular concert. They must write no letters to absent children, for they cannot afford the postage. They must never contribute anything to their church or chapel, or give any help to a neighbour which costs them money. They cannot save nor join sickness clubs or Trade Union, because they cannot pay the necessary subscriptions. The children must have no pocket money for dolls, marbles or sweets. The father must smoke no tobacco, and must drink no beer. The mother must never buy any pretty clothes for herself or for her children, the character of the family wardrobe as for the family diet, being governed by the regulation: 'nothing must be bought but that which is absolutely necessary.' "

Clearly much remained to be done in the twentieth century to improve the conditions of vast numbers of the working population. Two world wars inevitably held up housing reform, but as suburbs developed and new council estates were provided the masses have, on the whole, been able to enjoy greatly improved housing conditions.

It must be remembered however, that it was the increasing importance of working-class opinion that was responsible for much of the beneficial legislation. The Liberal Reforms before 1914 (such as Old Age Pensions, Labour Exchanges and National Insurance) were assisted by the votes of Labour MPs. These reforms ushered in the age of democracy in which there was an unceasing demand for better conditions for the masses. They also laid the foundation of what we call the welfare state. The movement towards equality, and the increase in the sphere of state action which it fostered, are trends that have continued to the present day, and have been the real achievement of the Rise of the Labour Movement.

Table of Events

1792	London Corresponding Society founded.
1793	Sheffield Society of Constitutional Information founded.
1811–16	Luddite riots.
1812	Primitive Methodist Church officially founded.
1816	Spa Fields riots.
1817	March of the Blanketeers; Derbyshire Insurrection.
1819	Peterloo Massacre.
1820	Cato Street Conspiracy.
1821	London Co-operative Society founded.
1825	Co-operative community founded at Orbiston.
1825–30	Early trade unions established.
1826–32	Swing riots.
1828	First edition of the *Co-operator* published.
1830	National Association for the Protection of Labour founded.
1831	National Union of the Working Classes founded.

1834	Grand National Consolidated Trades Union founded; Tolpuddle Martyrs.
1836	London Working Men's Association founded.
1837	People's Charter.
1839	Chartist Convention; Chartists' first petition presented to Parliament; Chartist rising in Monmouth.
1840	National Charter Association formed; *The Northern Star* first published.
1842	The second Chartist petition; the Plug Plot.
1844	The Rochdale Society of Equitable Pioneers founded.
1845	The Chartist Land Company formed.
1847	Feargus O'Connor elected to Parliament.
1848	The third Chartist petition; Christian Socialist Group formed.
1851	Amalgamated Society of Engineers founded.
1860	London Trades Council formed.
1862	Manhood Suffrage and Vote by Ballot Association formed.
1865	National Reform League founded.
1866	The Sheffield outrages.
1867	The Royal Commission on Trade Unions established.
1868	Hornby v Close case; first meeting of the TUC.
1869	Labour Representation League founded.
1871	Trade Union Act.
1872	Co-operative Wholesale Society founded.
1874	The first "Labour" MPs elected.
1883	Women's Co-operative Guild established.
1884	Social Democratic Federation founded; Socialist League founded; Fabian Society founded.
1887	"New Unionism" established.
1888	Dockers' strike; Scottish Labour Party founded.
1891	Labour Church established.
1893	Independent Labour Party founded.
1900	Labour Representation Committee formed.
1901	The Taff Vale case.
1906	The Labour Party formed.
1907	The Osborne case.
1910	The *Industrial Syndicalist* first published.

Dramatis Personae

WILLIAM ALLAN (1813–74). Secretary of the Amalgamated Society of Engineers. First full-time paid secretary of a trade union. Helped to found the London Trades Council in 1869. One of the Junta group which led the trade union movement for many years.

ROBERT APPLEGARTH (1834–1924). Secretary of the Amalgamated Society of Carpenters and Joiners, 1862. A member of the Junta and a key witness to the Royal Commission on Trade Unions in 1867.

JOSEPH ARCH (1826–1919). Agricultural labourer and Primitive Methodist local preacher. Founder and president of the National Agricultural Labourers' Union, 1872. Elected MP for NW Norfolk 1885–86 and 1892–1900.

THOMAS ATTWOOD (1783–1856). A banker who founded the Birmingham Political Union in 1830. MP for Birmingham 1832–39, and supported the Chartist Movement.

ANNIE BESANT (1847–1933). A member of the Fabian Society. In 1888, she organized support for the successful Match Girls' strike.

JOHN BURNS (1858–1943). Chairman of the TUC in 1892. MP from 1902, and as President of the Board of Trade in 1914 was the first working man to become a Cabinet Minister.

THOMAS BURT (1837–1922). A miner. MP for Morpeth 1874–1918.

JOHN DOHERTY (1797–1854). Imprisoned for strike activity in 1819. Formed Grand General Union of Operative Spinners in 1829 and the National Association for the Protection of Labour in 1830, in an attempt to unite all trades in one great union.

FRIEDRICH ENGELS (1820–95). A socialist friend of Karl Marx, one of the co-founders of international Communism and joint-author of *Das Kapital* and *The Communist Manifesto*.

KEIR HARDIE (1856–1915). Scottish miners' trade union leader. Strict Nonconformist and ardent socialist. Founder and Chairman of the Independent Labour Party in 1893. MP 1892–95, and 1900–15.

HENRY HUNT (1773–1835). "Orator Hunt", leading radical speaker. Imprisoned for his speech at the 1819 Peterloo Massacre.

HENRY HYNDMAN(1842–1921). Adopted and expounded the theories of Karl Marx, and founded the Social Democratic Foundation in 1884.

DR WILLIAM KING (1786–1865). A writer on co-operation and social questions. Edited an influential monthly periodical entitled the *Co-operator.*

GEORGE LOVELESS (1797–1874). Leader of the Dorset agricultural labourers (Tolpuddle Martyrs), who formed a trade union branch in 1834, and were sentenced to seven years' transportation.

WILLIAM LOVETT (1800–77). A cabinet maker who in 1830 became secretary of the British Association for Promoting Co-operative Knowledge. He assisted in the founding in 1836 of the London Working Men's Association and in drawing up the Six Points of the People's Charter. He was elected secretary of the 1839 Chartist Convention and was leader of the "Moral Force" Chartists. He wrote books on Chartism and education.

ALEXANDER MACDONALD (1821–81). Miners' leader who built up the Miners' National Union in 1873. One of the first two "Labour" MPs in 1874.

RAMSAY MACDONALD (1866–1937). Joined ILP in 1894. Helped to persuade trade unionists to assist in forming the Labour Party. Secretary of the Labour Representation Committee in 1900. Later Prime Minister of the first two Labour Governments.

TOM MANN (1856–1941). Leader of the successful Dockers' Strike in 1889. Became General Secretary of the Independent Labour Party.

KARL MARX (1818–83). German revolutionist, sociologist and economist, from whom the movement known as Marxism derives its name and ideas. Expelled from Germany and France, Marx went to London in 1849. He became the leading spirit of the International Working Men's Association. He was one of the co-founders of international Communism and joint-author of *Das Kapital* and *The Communist Manifesto*.

WILLIAM MORRIS (1834–96). Poet, artist and socialist. He founded the Socialist League in 1884.

FEARGUS O'CONNOR (1794–1855). Chartist leader, whose eloquence and enthusiasm gave him popularity, and whose paper, *The Northern Star*, did much to advance Chartism. Elected MP for Nottingham in 1847, but went insane in 1852.

ROBERT OWEN (1771–1858). Enlightened factory owner. His socialist and co-operative village schemes ended in practical failure. His Grand National Consolidated Trades Union of 1833 had but fleeting success.

GEORGE POTTER (1832–93). Editor of the labour paper *The Beehive* from 1861. Formed the LWMA in 1866.

JOSEPH RAYNOR STEPHENS (1805–79). A Wesleyan Methodist minister who resigned to agitate for factory reform and to become a zealous oratorical leader in the early years of the Chartist Movement.

WILL THORNE (1857–1945). Organized the Gas Workers' Union in 1887. He helped to found the National Association of General and Municipal Workers 1899, and was General Secretary of the Union 1889–1932. MP 1906–45.

BEN TILLETT (1860–1943). One of the leaders of the 1889 Dockers' Strike. MP 1917–24 and 1929–31.

List of Sources

(1) Quoted in C P Hill, *British Economic and Social History 1700—1939* (1970) p 15
(2) *Ibid*, p 14
(3) Rev D Davies, *The Case of the Labourers in Husbandry* (1795) p 55
(4) William Cobbett, *Rural Rides* (2 vols Everyman)
(5) *Child Labour in Factories, Parliamentary Commissioners Reports* (1833) XX 16
(6) William Cobbett, *Political Register* (November 1824)
(7) *Parliamentary Papers,* vol XCI (1842) p 295
(8) *First Report of Children's Employment Commission* vol XV (1842) p 71
(9) J Aikin, *A Description of the Country from thirty to forty miles around Manchester* (1795) p 192
(10) J P Kay, *The Moral and Physical Condition of the Working Classes in Manchester* (1832) p 12
(11) *Home Office Papers* 40/41
(12) Quoted in F Peel, *The Risings of the Luddites* (1895) p 12
(13) Quoted in L M Munby (ed), *The Luddites and Other Essays* (1971) p 122
(14) *Sherwin's Weekly Political Register* (18th August, 1819)
(15) Quoted in J Marlow, *The Peterloo Massacre* (1969) p 174
(16) Quoted in E J Hobsbawm and G Rude, *Captain Swing* (1969) p 156
(17) *Ibid*, p 137
(18) William Cobbett, *Political Register* (17th August, 1833)
(19) J Wade, *British History, Chronologically Arranged* (1839)
(20) A Chartist Handbill: quoted in G D H Cole and A W Filson, *British Working Class Movement, Select Documents 1789—1875* (1967) p 352
(21) *Leeds Mercury* (16th October, 1830)
(22) *Report of the Parliamentary Committee enquiring into the plight of the Handloom Weavers* (1875)
(23) Quoted in J T Ward, *Chartism* (1873) p 152
(24) *The Northern Star* (2nd February, 1839)
(25) *Hansard* 3/XL VIII/222
(26) Quoted in Max Beer, *A History of British Socialism* vol II, p 98
(27) *Ibid*, vol II, p 41
(28) *Ibid,* vol II, p 42–43
(29) Quoted in J T Ward, *op cit*, pp 172–173
(30) *The Northern Star* (August 1840)
(31) *Hansard* 3/13–90 (3rd May, 1842)
(32) *Ibid*, 2/XC VIII (March 1848)
(33) Quoted in J Savile, *Ernest Jones, Chartist* (1952) p 37
(34) Quoted in Thomas Carlyle, *Chartism* (1839)
(35) W Lovett, *Life and Struggles of William Lovett* (1876) (1967 edn) pp 41–42)
(36) Quoted in T W Mercer, *Dr William King and the Co-operator 1828–1830*, p 119
(37) W Lovett, *op cit*, p 72
(38) *Poor Man's Guardian* (1st September, 1832; 22nd September, 1832)
(39) F Engels, *The Conditions of the Working Class in England in 1844* (1892 edn) p 237
(40) Quoted in G J Holyoake, *History of the Rochdale Equitable Pioneers* (1859) p 11
(41) *The Co-operative News* (23rd November, 1872)
(42) Quoted in G Cole, *A*

Century of Co-operation (1944) p 216
(43) *The United Trades Co-operative Journal* (10th July, 1830)
(44) Quoted in H Pelling, *A History of British Trade Unionism* (1963) pp 31–32
(45) *The Times* (20th March, 1834)
(46) Quoted in Cole and Filson, *op cit,* p 478
(47) *The Times* (12th January, 1852)
(48) *The Trades Union Commission: Sheffield Outrages Inquiry* (1867) Interim Report, pp 7–8
(49) *The Eleventh Report of the Royal Commission on Trade Unions* (1869) p 19
(50) *Proceedings of the National Conference of Miners* (1875) p 13, quoted in Cole and Filson, *op cit*, pp 501–2
(51) *The Autobiography of Joseph Arch* (1966) pp 46–47
(52) *Parliamentary Papers* vol XIV (1882) p 91
(53) Will Thorne, *My Life's Battles* (1924) pp 76–77
(54) *The Times* (16th September, 1889)
(55) *Ibid* (13th September, 1910)
(56) W V Osborne, *My Case* (1910) p 39
(57) Tom Mann, *Memoirs* (1923) p 252
(58) *Ibid*, p 255
(59) F Engels, *op cit*, p 125
(60) S S Henshaw, *The Romance of our Schools* (1910) pp 10 and 25
(61) *Primitive Methodist Magazine* (1833) pp 2–3
(62) *Primitive Methodist Preachers' Magazine* (1832)
(63) *Minutes of the Primitive Methodist Conference 1819,* p 5
(64) W Booth, *How to Reach the Masses with the Gospel* (1872) p 71
(65) *Labour Prophet* (1892) p 4 and (1893) p 76
(66) *The Labour Prophet* (January 1893). See E J Hobsbawm (ed), *Labour's Turning Point 1880–1900* (1948) p 141
(67) *Reynolds' Newspaper* (23rd November, 1862)
(68) Joseph Irving, *The Annals of our Time* (1871)
(68) Quoted in R Harrison, *Before the Socialists* (1965) p 89
(70) Quoted in A W Humphrey, *A History of Labour Representation* (1912)
(71) Quoted in Cole and Filson, *op cit*, pp 588–89
(72) Karl Marx, *The Communist Manifesto* (1948) pp 13–15
(73) Quoted in E J Hobsbawm (ed), *Labour's Turning Point 1880–1900* (1948) pp 46–47
(74) Tom Mann, *Memoirs* (1967) pp 25–27
(75) Quoted in J B Glasier, *William Morris and the Early Days of the Socialist Movement* (1921) p 32
(76) Quoted in W Stewart, *J Keir Hardie: a biography* (1921) p 24
(77) *Ibid*, p 41
(78) Quoted in J Cockburn, *The Hungry Heart: A Romantic Biography of James Keir Hardie* (1956) pp 118–21
(79) *Annual Register* (1893) p 8
(80) Quoted in G R Smith, *The Rise of the Labour Party in Great Britain* (1969) p 33
(81) G B Shaw, *Fortnightly Review* (1st November, 1893)
(82) Quoted in Pauline Gregg, *A Social and Economic History of Britain 1760–1965* (1965 edn) p 400
(83) The *Clarion* (10th March, 1900)
(84) Quoted in Bill Simpson, *Labour, the Unions and the Party* (1973)

Further Reading

General

G D H Cole, *A Short History of the British Working Class Movement 1787—1947* (Allen and Unwin 1925)

G D H Cole and R Postgate, *The British Common People 1746—1946* (Methuen 1961)

E P Thompson, *The Making of the English Working Class* (Penguin 1968)

Documentary

G D H Cole and A W Filson (eds), *British Working Class Movements, Select Documents 1789—1875* (Macmillan 1967)

P Hollis (ed), *Class and Conflict in 19th Century England 1815—1850* (Routledge 1973)

Early Radical Movements

F O Darvall, *Popular Disturbances and Public Order in Regency England* (Oxford University Press 1969)

E J Hobsbawm and G Rude, *Captain Swing* (Lawrence and Wishart 1969)

M I Thomis, *The Luddites: Machine-Breaking in Regency England* (David and Charles 1970)

Chartism

A Briggs (ed), *Chartist Studies* (Macmillan 1963)

G D H Cole, *Chartist Portraits* (Macmillan 1941, 1965)

C Thorne, *Chartism* (Macmillan 1966)

J T Ward, *Chartism* (Batsford 1973)

Co-operation

G D H Cole, *A Century of Co-operation* (Allen and Unwin 1944)

R G Garnett, *Co-operation and the Owenite Socialist Communities in Britain 1825—45* (Manchester University Press 1972)

Trade Unions

E H Hobsbawm, *Labouring Men* (Weidenfeld 1964)

A E Musson, *British Trade Unions 1800—1875* (Longmans 1972)

H Pelling, *A History of British Trade Unionism* (Penguin 1963)

Religion and the Working Class

K S Inglis, *Churches and the Working Classes in Victorian England* (Routledge and Kegan Paul 1963)

S Mayor, *The Churches and the Labour Movement* (Independent Press 1967)

R F Wearmouth, *The Social and Political Influence of Methodism in the Twentieth Century* (Epworth 1957)

Socialism and the Labour Movement

P Adelman, *The Rise of the Labour Party 1880—1945* (Longmans 1972)

G D H Cole, *British Working Class Politics 1832—1914* (Routledge 1941)

H Pelling, *The Origins of the Labour Party 1880—1900* (Macmillan 1954)

Biographies

J Arch (Ed J G O'Leary), *The Autobiography of Joseph Arch* (MacGibbon and Kee 1966)

G D H Cole, *The Life of Robert Owen* (Cass 1965)

T Mann, *Tom Mann's Memoirs* (MacGibbon and Kee 1967)

Fiction

Several nineteenth-century novels throw light on various features and struggles of the British labouring class. For example:

Charles Dickens, *Bleak House, Oliver Twist, Hard Times*

Benjamin Disraeli, *Sybil*

Mrs Gaskell, *Mary Barton*

Charles Kingsley, *The Water Babies*

Index

Picture Credits

The author and publishers wish to thank the following for the pictures which appear in this book:
The Co-operative Union Library 48, 52, 54 (right); Labour Party Library 23, 30, 59, 64, 65, 75, 79 (right), 81, 101, 103, 107, 113; Mansell Collection 21, 26, 27, 35 (right), 35 (bottom), 36, 37, 41, 43, 53, 67; Radio Times Hulton Picture Library 11, 18, 24, 32 (left and right), 35 (left), 45, 46, 49, 54(left), 55, 57, 70, 76, 78, 79(left), 82(left and right), 85, 94, 96, 100(right); TUC Library 19, 62, 68(left and right), 69, 72, 73, 89, 100(left), 111, 115; The remainder of the pictures are from the Wayland Picture Library.